THE MAKING OF A BLENDED FAMILY

PASTOR JERRY Q. PARRIES

xulon PRESS

The Making of a Blended Family
Blended Family
by Pastor Jerry Q Parries

Printed in the United States of America.

ISBN 9781498493390

www.xulonpress.com

Forward By
JaMice Lewis
My Daughter

S uddenly in the summer 1993 we were a blended family. Jerry Q Parries moved in and Jayson and Justin were coming up for the summer. We had just left my childhood home and moved into a three bedroom apartment in another city. Away from my friends, parents were getting a divorce and "bam" now I have two brothers and a new dad? Forming that into a sentence today pretty much sums up my attitude about the whole thing. I was angry, confused and shocked and I showed it towards my new family.

I spent about 7 years being mean and hateful. 7 years of being disrespectful, but despite all of that you always loved me. You were always kind and still took my hateful self on vacation. This blended family wasn't by far easy and it took over ten years for me to claim you as my father and to love you as such.

I pray this book blesses blended families and gives them the tools to be successful.

In turn my advice to my blended families be patient with one another and introduce your future mate and their kids early and gradually allow them to form a relationship.

Dedication

I would like to dedicate this book to my wife, Eunice, without whom this book would never been written. To our children, Jayson, Jamice, Justin, and Ryan, thank you for standing with your Mother, - Bonus/Mother and me as we did our best to become one family. I would also like to thank the mother and father of our children, Sandra and James, for being such great parents. To the grandmothers, grandfathers, aunts, and uncles who love our family, thanks for your support. To all of our grandchildren, who we love dearly, this book is dedicated to you. To everyone in a blended family who have done the hard work to keep it together, we dedicate this book to you and your family.

Now unto him that is able to keep you from falling, and
to present you faultless before the presence of his glory
with exceeding joy, to the only wise God our Saviour, be
glory and majesty, dominion and power,
both now and ever. Amen.
Jude 1:24-25 (KJV)

Table of Contents

Introduction

What have I learned about blended families? I've lived in one all of my life. I was born into one; I created one. I want to share my experiences and the lessons I have learned with you. What you will read comes from my childhood and many years living in my own blended family, created with my wife, Eunice. I am convinced what I am going to share with you will help you navigate through the maze of being in a blended family.

Here's what I can tell you right off the bat. If you hope to have any success in making it with a blended family, I believe you need to have God at the center of your foundation. I believe your faith should be in Jesus Christ and that He is the rock you should build on. I am not writing this book from a Christian perspective only; what I share will be practical life lessons. These lessons can be used in a Christian home or a non-Christian home. I believe, however, I was only able to do the things I have done because

I had a greater power than myself to love and forgive me in challenging times. I encourage you to have a greater power in your life if you are going to be able to succeed in blending your family together.

My advice stems from what has worked for me as well as what has worked for others. Over the last ten years, I have helped many couples through some challenging times as they built their new marriages and new families. Some of these people made it and others did not invest the hard work necessary to win the battle. Those who listened were able to come out on the other side. Those who refused to humble themselves ultimately ended up with a failed marriage and broken homes. I hope this will not be the case in your life. Blended families can work and I am a witness that it can happen.

How did we pull it together and become one family? This book will tell you. You'll discover how to do it yourself. If you follow my directions, you too can have a happy and successful blended family. Be not deceived; this will take a lot of work and patience. You will hear me say over and over again throughout this book that a blended family is very, very hard work.

I suggest you read this book with your partner and discuss each chapter. Use the stories I share to help you to walk through the issues. Be honest. Some of the things I ask you to do are very hard but let your partner know to be patient with you in these areas. Here is one thing I like to say when I am talking to couples:

"Your truth is your truth, but it may not be ultimate truth."

If you make your truth the ultimate truth, you shut out your partner's input into your problems. In my experience this will cause another problem—you thinking you are always right. In a marriage, there is always more than one way to see a situation. If you approach your issues understanding you may not be 100% right, you leave room for conversation.

I hope this book will open up a dialogue between you and your spouse so you can get on the same page to build not just a good blended family but an incredible one.

CHAPTER 1

I Know of What I Speak

"F.A.M.I.L.Y. is one of the strongest words anyone can say,
because the letters of FAMILY means Father
And Mother I Love You!"
Author Unknown

I have learned so much of what to do and what not to do when it comes to blended families as a result of my personal history. I was born into the middle of a blended family in 1961 and I had no choice in the matter. I was the baby boy of nine children. My dad brought one son from a previous marriage to his marriage to my mother and my mom brought three girls of her own. As a family, they had six more children together. Years later my parents divorced and my mother remarried, having two more children.

I saw my family as a normal, traditional family but we were anything but one. We were a blended family in every sense of the word. My dad was much older than my mom.

My father was a very kind and loving man however, his family did not seem to be very pleased with him marrying a younger woman with children. After all, he had been married a few times and by now it appeared his family had no confidence or trust in his abilities to choose a partner. They had no energy or interest in investing into another one of his new relationships. The way I saw it my dad's family may have been somewhat embarrassment and shied away from his new wife seeing that she was much younger and very beautiful. This was the 1950's and things where a bit different in those days. My mother, on the other hand, being young could have been perceived by my dad's family as a woman looking for a man to support her and her children. I am sharing this information to point out the dynamics of what takes place in a blended family.

My mother's family, however, seemed to support her decision to marry my father at least by the time I was born. Her sisters and brothers were very loving to us and we grew up hanging around their children.

I did not know we were a blended family; my mom and dad did an excellent job of not showing a difference between the children. They did this so well I did not know my dad was not my older sisters' biological father until many, many years later. I think I was around eleven or twelve when our family began to fall apart that I discovered that my dad was raising step daughters. The word "step" was never used in our home; the way I saw it we were one family.

In the early years of my life, my mom and dad were very committed to the church and we were raised up in it, singing in the choir. My mother was a musician for the church and everyone treated my family with love and respect. For the most part, we were welcomed and supported as a family. In the 50's blended families were not very common and still somewhat frowned upon, so support for our family from the church was needed and welcomed. The church was a place where others rallied around our family and helped keep us together. Our faith in Jesus Christ was huge and we needed this faith in a major way. Our faith in God was the glue that held my family together.

That all changed in 1970 when the pastor of our church said he was moving to Buffalo, NY. Our world as a family came crashing down. The church voted for a new pastor and many of the members were not happy. When the outcome did not go the way some wanted, the church split. My mother and father left the church and all hell broke loose in our family. We lost the one thing that was holding our family together and my mother seem to have lost faith in God and the church community. At least that was the way I saw it from an eleven year old boy's eyes. One day we loved Jesus and the next day our family was in chaos.

For the next few years, my mother and dad talked about getting a divorce. To this day, I am not sure what took place. It seems as if we left the church and the enemy launched an attack to destroy our family and the children by any means necessary. Without Jesus being the center of our family life, our family started spinning out of control. My parent's marriage began to unravel and the children were getting ready to pay a huge price for their decisions. My parents began to argue intensely in our home, shattering the foundation that once offered safe haven from the outside .

My mother and father divorced, both of them remarried, and our lives were forever changed. Both of my parents' new partners were not involved in our lives. As a young child, I not only lost my family to the divorce, I lost my mother and father to new relationships we were not invited to. This is not a way to blend a family together.

The first lesson I learned about living as a blended family is that you must forgive much, love much, and apologize often. I hold no ill feelings toward anyone for what I went through as a child. It is because of those experiences I am writing this book in the hopes of helping someone else. Forgiveness is a powerful tool that can heal the broken hearted and set the captives free.

I believe the results growing up in a broken home at such an early age led me to move to Memphis, TN seeking family, getting married at eighteen years old. I was running from a painful, broken family with no place to turn, trying to start a family life for which I had longed. Two wonderful sons were born of that union. I remain married to my first wife for about seven years and then we divorced. Even though it appeared like I was repeating what I had experienced as a child, I wanted to make sure that my sons remained top priority in my life. I was single but I came with kids; any person interested in me had to take the entire package. I was determined not to repeat for my children my past experience. I made sure any woman I spoke to knew they would have to receive my children if they wanted to be with me.

I met my wife Eunice in 1990. She had two wonderful children and I understood she came as a package deal. We started dating, subsequently we married and our journey of blending our families together began.

Most of what I share in this book I've had firsthand experience dealing with; lessons from my parents, what I've learned from my previous marriage, and what I am learning and experiencing now.

CHAPTER 2

What Is a Blended Family?

"The love of a family is life's greatest blessing"
Author Unknown

A blended family includes children from the previous marriage of the wife, husband, or both parents. It is when you take two families and make them into one. One of the most famous blended families in the early seventies had a song that went like this.

Here's the story of a lovely lady who was
bringing up three very lovely girls.
All of them had hair of gold, like their mother,
the youngest one in curls.

Here's the story, of a man named Brady, who
was busy with three boys of his own

They were four men, living all together, yet they were all alone.

Till the one day when the lady met this fellow and they knew it was much more than a hunch, That this group must somehow form a family. That's the way we all became the Brady Bunch.

©*The Brady Bunch Lyrics by Frank DeVol and Sherwood Schwartz*

The Brady Bunch made it look so easy. What my wife and I did not know was the work, and I mean WORK it takes to make a successful blended family happen. I think blended families were never meant to be; marriage was designed to last forever. However, in this day and time, blended families have become the norm. Here are the statistics of marriages:

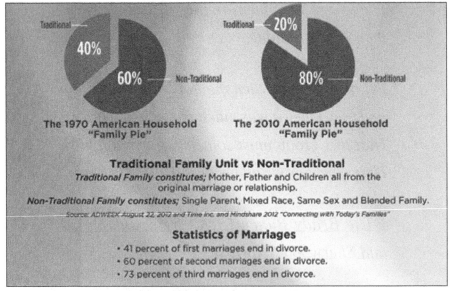

The 1970 American Household "Family Pie"

The 2010 American Household "Family Pie"

Traditional Family Unit vs Non-Traditional

Traditional Family constitutes; Mother, Father and Children all from the original marriage or relationship.

Non-Traditional Family constitutes; Single Parent, Mixed Race, Same Sex and Blended Family.

Source: ADWEEK August 22, 2012 and Time inc. and Mindshare 2012 "Connecting with Today's Families"

Statistics of Marriages

- 41 percent of first marriages end in divorce.
- 60 percent of second marriages end in divorce.
- 73 percent of third marriages end in divorce.

Source ADWEEK August 22 2012 and Time Inc.
and Mindshare 2012 Connecting with Today's Families

Let's look at the things you must consider before choosing a partner with which to blend your family. If there is one thing you must do, it is to look for a partner who understands your children are the most important people to you. Once you find a partner willing to receive everything that comes with you, you have the beginnings of building a healthy blended family. This is just the beginning; there is still a lot of ground work that must take place.

Let's assume your partner has children as well. (If there are no children some of these steps will not apply to your situation.) Both people must consider their ex-spouses. Although you are not marrying these ex-spouses, they will be a great influence in your new marriage. How are the relationships with your ex-spouses? How does your ex's feel about their child being around a new person? Do they want their child to call another person Mom or Dad? These are questions you should be able to answer before you enter into a new marriage because children are involved.

The answers to these questions will have a profound effect on the new life you are building. Whatever relationship your partner has with their ex will affect your blended family in some way. Please don't think you can marry your partner and not deal with the ex-spouses at some point and time.

Another point to consider in the relationship is any extended family. Let's say John and Mary were married for ten years and have recently gotten a divorce. John meets a new woman named Helen and is thinking about creating a new family with Helen. However his first wife, Mary, is very close to John's parents and immediate family. John's family intent is to continue to welcome Mary as a family member. Will Helen be able to handle Mary being a part of John's family on a continuous basis? These are the real dynamics you need to take into consideration when choosing a partner. For example, how close is the relationship between Mary and John's immediate family? Something like this may not cause a problem for your new relationship, however, you need to understand what you are about to enter into.

Don't forget, when you join into a new relationship, you need to meet your partner's children's aunts and uncles so they will be supportive of your new position in the family. These relatives have an invested interest in the lives of their nieces and nephews to see them become well-rounded adults. Depending on the family, you may see these people at programs, events, and school functions throughout the adolescent life of your children. Just because your new partner did not get along with their former spouse, don't assume that their family will kick that former spouse to the curb and automatically move you into their position. Depending on how long the ex has been a part of the family, you may have to win the family over to receiving you.

As an example, my wife's brother was married to his first wife for many years. When they divorced, she remained in the same position with my wife's family. Even though my brother-in-law and his wife have been divorced over twenty-five years, and his new wife has been welcomed into the family, his new wife must deal with his ex as part of the extended family's unspoken agreement. Why? Because his children love their mother and they want everyone to share all their important days together as family. Dynamics such as these are real and must be talked about BEFORE you walk down the aisle.

Another factor to consider is how loyal children are to their biological parents and how often they will rebel against the person you have chosen as your new spouse. Your new partner has to learn how to win them over without pulling the "I'm the man/woman of this house card." the person who uses this kind of tactic will ultimately lose the blended family

How It Worked For Me

Let me share more about my blended family and how it came to be. I had been divorced for about four years when I met Eunice. My youngest son was seven and my oldest son was nine. My two sons lived with their mother in Memphis, TN. Even though I lived in Cleveland, OH, I was a dad fully engaged in the lives of my children. Every summer and Christmas holiday the children came to be with me.

Eunice comes to the relationship with two children as well; her youngest child was a five year old boy and her oldest was an eight year old girl. Both children loved their biological dad very much and he was also completely engaged in their lives and they shared joint custody of the children.

As long as my wife and I were together, with no outside influence from our children or extended family, things were excellent. However, when her children came home from their dad's house and my children came from Memphis major adjustments had to be made. For the sake of identifying who I am speaking about, I am going to say my stepchildren but I caution to say this is a term that should *never* be used in your blended family.

From the very first day I came into my wife's life, my stepdaughter was not fond of me. It had nothing to do with me at all; she was a daddy's girl and, because she was loyal to him, I was the enemy. I was young and stupid, and took it personally when it was not personal at all. Since she froze me out, I did not show her the love she needed. My stepdaughter was doing what was natural—protecting her dad's position in her heart.

My wife's young son was no different. Boys are naturally very close to their mothers; this is why most men are "mama's boys". When a new man comes into the house of a single woman, sons are generally very suspicious of the man because by nature they see themselves as the protectors of their mother. Again, with Eunice's son, I took this action as an attack against me personally. I recognize now it was a God-given defense mechanism since we are all born with the desire to protect the ones we love. Do you see the tension that came into our home just from coming together as a blended family? No one had done anything wrong but instead we were all experiencing natural feelings.

In the summer, we added my two sons to the mix and things became even more complicated. My youngest son, remember, is a "mama's boy" so when he comes to the house he is still protecting her position in his heart. He did not warm up to the new lady in his life (my wife) and, in fact, had a hard time feeling any connection with her. Again, because we did not have a mentor in this matter, my wife took it personally when it had nothing to do with her at all. My son simply felt he needed to remain committed to his mom and did not comprehend how to make room for another mom at this time.

My oldest son unusually is a "daddy's boy." Interestingly, he felt the need to negotiate everything on my behalf to make sure I was getting the best deal out of my relationship with this new lady. His stepping in caused my wife to tell him often she was not speaking to him and to stay out of grown folk's conversations.

What was happening? All of our children were watching out for their parents' interests which manifested through their actions.

Although our kids played well together, there was another family dynamic lurking in the dark. My baby boy was no longer the baby of the family. My stepson was the new baby of the family and my wife made it known to the dismay of all of the children. Most of these dynamics in a traditional family would not be giving a second thought, however in a blended family we are sensitive to the needs of our own children and our children use these sensitivities to play on the emotions of the biological parents. Everything my wife and I did had the potential to be scrutinized better not show any partiality between the kids. Most children take cues from their parents and will use this to drive a wedge between them for the sole purpose of getting their young needs met. I don't believe kids are thinking about destroying the relationship but I believe they are trying to have free course to accomplish their wants. Sometime children will use the stepparent as the cause of their discomfort when they are been denied their wants. My wife and I had to learn what a legitimate grievance was and what was a play on our emotions.

Today, I am happy to say after twenty-six years of hard work we are all still together, loving on each other. My oldest son and daughter live here in Orlando with their families. My son lives in Memphis, and the youngest son lives in Cleveland with their family. We now have around ten grandchildren and our adult children are dealing with their own blended families. From time to time, we still have issues come up just like any traditional family would have. However, we know that with love and forgiveness there is nothing you can't conquer.

CHAPTER 3

Choose a Partner Wisely

"When it comes to choosing between life and death, choose wisely.
The wrong choice could create consequences for others."
Author Unknown

There are qualities you need to look for when searching for a partner that would be a good candidate for a blended family. There are things that could and should raise red flags should you see them in the person you are interested in. Do not dismiss the concerns you see or think you have the power to change the person in the future. Sometime we only look on the outside appearance of a person to make a decision concerning a partner.

Let me assure you in blending a family it takes great communication and negotiation skills to make the union successful. Looks alone will not sustain the necessary skills needed to execute this goal. It is best to set aside superficial

27

criteria, such as looks, body type, popularity, fame, fortune, etc., that impede our judgment for good common sense.

Allow me to share this bit of advice. Never introduce your children to your new partner until you are sure the relationship will be a permanent one. After you have been dating for a while and you are sure that this person is the one, then it is time to meet the family. If the person you are seeing refuses to introduce you to their family, it is a red flag and you should be very, very cautious about moving the relationship forward.

The Search for a Good Man

Let us start the search for a good partner. What should one look for in the man? Ladies, in making a good decision in finding a great partner, you first want to look and assess his family dynamics. You should want to know about his interactions with his mother, father, sisters, and brothers because his treatment of them is an indication on how he will be with you. Look to see how he responds to the ones that are closest to him. What kind of relationship does he have with them?

You should also ask if he is a product of a broken home or a blended family. You want to explore and understand the dynamics of his entire family. Does he have stepbrothers or stepsisters he grew up with and how is his relationship with them? These questions are important to ask and have answered in order to understand his views of a blended family. Was his stepmother and/or stepfather kind to him? How does he feel about the relationship now with his own parents? What did he learn from his experiences with them and how will this be different in your relationship? Don't be afraid to have these conversations at the beginning of the relationship. How his family has interacted with him will be his reference point to deal with a blended family with you. By no means am I suggesting if he had a bad experience he would be a bad father or husband; however, it is a good place to understand what he learned from these experiences.

As you continue to interact with his family, pay close attention to how he interacts to the people closest to him. Listen and watch how he speaks to the women of his life. Is he kind to his mother? Does he cater to her needs? When she asks him a question, does he respond respectfully? When you first meet a man never, ever look at how they treat you. They are putting forth their best effort to win you over. If he doesn't respect his mother or sisters, it is a good indication he will not respect you. A man who honors his mother will honor his wife in most cases. Of course, there are no guarantees, but the foundation is there. Look to see if his dad takes good care of his mother with love, kindness, and honor; that will have been the model for him in his life. If a man's father is not in the home, he can still learn these skills from his mother and could be a great father. However the best teacher of a man is his father and in most cases he will model his life after him.

Another place to pay close attention is when he takes you out to dinner, how does he treat the waitress? If he gives the waitress his full attention when she is speaking to him, it is a good indication he will give you his full attention when he speaks to you. If he blows off the waitress when she is speaking, it is a good indication he will blow you off in the future. See how he responds when he has to send his food back to the kitchen. Does he demand a redo or does he kindly ask that it be prepared the way he ordered it? Pay attention to everything and see if he goes off on the manager or graciously except his or her apology. If he is gracious to others, he will be gracious to you. If he ignores and blows off others, this is an insight into the way he may eventually treat you. All the signs you need are right in front of you; watch and listen and you will learn what kind of person you are inviting into your life. Here is a good way to understand his personality; listen to him when he talks on the phone. How is his tone and demeanor with the person he is speaking with? If you listen and watch, you will quickly know the kind of person he really is at his core.

Is he soft spoken? Did he handle the person on the phone in a disrespectful way? What did he say when he hung up the phone? What were his comments? Listen to what he says about other person after the call as this may be what he may say about you when you are not around. If you want to find out how a person really is, never watch how they treat you but see how they treat others.

While looking at the dynamics of his family and watching how he treats others, you also need to pay attention to his personal life. Inquire about what happened to his previous relationships. How long has it been since he was divorced or ended his last relationship? Remember, he needs time to heal from his ex so he is not using you as a rebound. What did he learn from the last relationship that will help him in his new partnership with you? These are the questions you need to ask to gather all the information you need to have a successful relationship with him. What you are searching for with these types of questions is what may have been the cause of his last relationship's failure so you will not repeat it. You want to make sure that if he contributed in any way, he has learned from those mistakes. The more he is willing to admit he contributed in some ways to the demise of his last relationship, the more you will see if he is a man who takes responsibility for his actions. If he blames the entire demise of the relationship on the woman, or even his family, that should be a red flag for you. Please don't be blinded by love and not open your eyes to the things that will help you make a good decision. After you understand the history of your new partner, you are well on your way to having the information needed to make a wise decision.

You should also ask if he has any children and, if so, how many and by who. This is crucial if you have children. You need to see how he is dealing with his kids to determine if and how he will deal with your children. If he is a good father to his own children, he will likely be a good father to yours. If he is an absent father to his own children, it is a strong indication he may not deal with your children in a healthy way. If a man won't take care of his current family, he will not take care of a new one.

If a man takes care of another woman's children, and not his own, his biological children may have animosity against their father. That animosity will spill over to you and your family. A healthy blended family allows him to bring his children into his new family in a way that allows him to continue to raise his children in a loving, positive environment.

If there are no red flags and only if your relationship is truly serious, you should seek to meet the ex-wife or former partner if children are involved. Why, you ask? Every parent wants to know who their children are going to be around. This is a natural curiosity and defense mechanism; a woman wants to protect her children. It is a reasonable request or demand from the ex. Without a doubt, you may receive baby mama drama at the beginning because no one wants their kids around their ex's new romantic interest. This is a normal reaction. Hopefully, as the ex sees you love their child, she will be ok with the relationship. This may take time to work out so you must be patient. I would suggest the mother drop her children at the house at some point so she can see where her children will be staying; she is more likely then to feel comfortable releasing her children into your hands. Again this level of trust takes time; be open to allow this to happen naturally.

If your new partner has deceived his ex in anyway, and it is the reason they are no longer together, you may experience the repercussions of their unresolved issues. I suggest you find out what happened from your new partner so you can prevent the same thing from happening to you. If your new partner has children by more than one woman, your future blended family has just become a little more challenging. It is not impossible, but it is going to take a lot more work due to the fact you have two or more women to deal with.

With this in mind, you should examine how he is providing for his children. Does the state take out his child support payments and, if so, how much? When you marry him you are joining yourself to that obligation? This will have an effect on your ability to properly take care of your household. Don't be blinded by love and think none of this concerns you; it all concerns you and will be a part of your life forever. Don't think that when the kids turn eighteen years old he will be through with them. Are you through with you mother and father? I am over fifty years old and I still deal with my children's mother because we have grandbabies which we both love dearly. When you blend a family together, it is a life time commitment.

The Search for a Good Woman

How should you pick a good woman to partner? Everything shared above applies to the case of looking for a good woman as well. Men are attracted by what they see, so they have a tendency to look at the outward appearance first. Remember that hit song in the late seventies by the Commodores:

She's a brick house, she's mighty, mighty, and
just lettin' it all hang out
She knows she's got everything, that a woman
needs to get a man

How can she lose with the sex she use 36-24-
36, what a winning hand

She's a brick house, she's mighty, mighty....

*Songwriters: LIONEL RICHIE, MILAN WILLIAMS, RONALD
LAPREAD, THOMAS MCCLARY, WALTER ORANGE,
WILLIAM KING © Sony/ATV Music Publishing LLC*

Every man wanted one of these ladies in his life. I want you to set aside, however, these superficial qualities. You need to look at the deeper qualities necessary to create a blended family for a lifetime. If you want to go into this new relationship long term, it should be your goal to make this round a lifetime commitment.

There are a few things that men commonly have a tendency to overlook because they are focusing on the wrong things. The first area you should give attention to is how the woman of your future honors the father in her life. If there is no father in her home, see how she speaks about her brothers or uncles. This is a great indication of how she feels about men in general. If you have the opportunity, try to have a conversation with her mother to see how her mother feels about men in general. If her mother speaks highly about her daughter's father, this could be a good sign. If her mother, however, subscribes to the notion that all men are dogs, then you may have some challenges ahead. You can rest assured her mother has tried to instill her feelings about men into her daughter. A woman learns how to treat a man based on the way her mother treated her father. No matter what her mother feels, it does not always mean that your new love feels the same way, but it is in the back of her mind, good or bad.

Since you are bringing your children into this union, please pay attention to the way she interacts with her children. If the grandmother is always babysittting her daughter's children while their mother is out, it should be a red flag for you. If your new partner will not be responsible to her own children, she may not be a good caregiver for your children. Women have an instinct to be mothers. If she doesn't fulfill that natural instinct with her biological children, she may not be capable of being sensitive to your children's needs. If her children are not top priority, it can be an indication she is self-centered, self-gratifying, and an otherwise selfish individual. You need to open your eyes to all of the signs. When you first meet a woman like this, you are absolutely blown away because she is fully engaged in you. Her attention, however, will likely go to the next thing; as she has neglected her children, she will neglect you. As she moves on, she will not be thinking about the blended family she is leaving behind.

Ask about the children's father; see how she speaks to you about him. Does she lift him up as a great father or cover his lack of involvement in his children life? If she puts him down, especially in front of her children, she may not be a wise choice to create a family with due to fact that she will not honor the father of her child. When the father wants to pick up the children for the weekend, does she cooperate with him? Does she make the transition easy or does she run him through the ringer and make it difficult for him to share in his children's life? Remember, don't look at how people treat you; look at how they treat others. This is the way they really behave and you will receive this kind of treatment when the honeymoon period is over. Listen to how she speaks to the children when they return home and see if she lifts their father up in their eyes or tears him down. If she lifts him up, she is someone you want to make a life with in the future. This is an indication she knows how to forgive and not hold grudges. This will work in your favor as you build a future together.

Also look at how she is dealing with child support. Is she being fair or is she trying to take him to the bank? A good woman will do what is fair and still try to help her children maintain a healthy relationship with the father. Regardless of the differences with the children's father, the woman you want to hold on to is one that promotes unity with the father's family.

It is just as important to inquire about her last relationship to learn what happened and why it was not successful. Whatever the reason the relationship did not work, ask what role she played that may have contributed to the relationship's demise. This is important to see if she has taken a look at herself and replayed the decisions that were made. You also need to talk about the level of involvement she will continue to have with her ex's family. Those children have extended relatives that are going to want to be a part of their lives. If the woman has children by more than one man, this process must be repeated with each guy so the children can grow up in as healthy an environment as possible. The more people you have to blend into this family, the more patient you will need to be to make it successful.

Questions for Both Sexes

These are just a few things men and women can look at in searching for a lifetime partner. If you are looking for a Christian person, you need to become a Christian yourself first, join a local church, and get connected. One of the mistakes a lot of people make is finding their partner in a club and later becoming upset that they will not attend church with the family. If you are looking for a five course meal, you do not go searching for it at McDonalds. When looking for a Christian partner, it is important for you to associate in the places those people are hanging out. My suggestion is to never find a partner in a club if you want him to be in the choir. The reverse is also true; never find a partner in the church if you like to live in the club. Have these conversations so you will know as much as possible about the other person and who they associate with. Our mothers told us the truth: "birds of a feather flock together." Your partner is more likely to be like the type of people they hang around.

Be willing to ask the hard questions. Don't forget to ask about medical reports; does the person have anything they need to expose? I know a story of a woman who married a man who did not tell her he had a heart condition. Less than one year after the wedding, he informed her that he needed a heart transplant. She wanted to know why he hadn't told her about the condition; his response was that it had never came up. This is an example of something you want to share with your partner voluntarily. She promptly divorced him because she felt totally deceived. Now, I am not saying you should tell someone everything that has ever happen to you in your life, however, if what is in your past could affect your life in the future, your partner has a right to know.

You also should ask to see your partner's credit report and ask about debts, credit card usage, or bankruptcy. Ask about everything you can think of in a tactful way. All of these things are fair questions to ask so you will know what you are getting into. Open your eyes, choose wisely, and pay attention to the way your intended treats others. When the honeymoon is over, this is the way they are going to treat you.

CHAPTER 4

Understanding Family Dynamics

"There are no foolish questions, only foolish silence."
Unknown

"He who knows all the answers has not yet been
asked all the questions"
Unknown

It is easy to think "I am marrying my new partner, not their family." This is so far from the truth. When you join to create a blended family together, you are joining everyone that has a connection to the children and your partner. Just because your partner's ex did not get along with your partner does not mean that the ex's family won't want to have some parts in the lives of the children. Many of these people have become a family to the ex and will highly influence how the children view your new relationship. This may not be the case for every situation, however, I have known a lot of cases were the ex remained a part of the family in some way. It takes a lot of grace to deal with these issues.

Let's look at the diagram below, which may be hard to follow. Donald is marrying April; she is a kind, sweet, and a wonderful soulmate. However, April has a lot of history that will be carried over into her new future. Donald has his own history as well, but we will look at one side for simplicity's sake although everything applies to both sides. A marriage like this is durable but it will be hard to manage. Study the diagram below so as you continue to read it will be easier to follow.

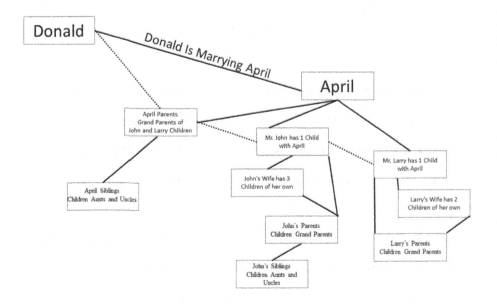

April has two children by two different men; their names are John and Larry. Both these men are now remarried with blended families representing five additional children who interact with April's children. Remember, whatever goes on in the houses of John and Larry will be brought home to April's house. (Do not deceive yourself that the influences of those other children will not affect April's children—they will. Some of those influences will be good and other will be against April's values.)

April's children have two set of grandparents—April's family and the father's family. April's children also have a host of uncles, aunts, and cousins. All of these people have a profound effect on the children, which will come back to April's home.

Here is April's family dynamics. April's parents are very much in love with their grandchildren and want to make sure they are given the best care. (Some grandparents are more intense about their grandchildren than they were about their own children.) They have an invested interest in the well-being of their grandbabies. They have put together a college fund and have opened up a small savings account to assure a great future for them. In the past, April may not have made the best choices concerning relationships, however, she has learned a great deal from her mistakes and has found the right guy this time.

Donald is introduced to April's family but is received with some skepticism and reservation. Donald must know this has nothing to do with him; the family's reservation is based on April's past history. Donald should be prepared to give April's family the space and time needed to welcome him into the fold. The way Donald responds to these moments will set the tone for many years to come. If Donald is going to rise to the occasion, he should consider doing these things:

A. Show April's family he is committed to loving her and making her happy.
B. Show love to April's children as his very own.
C. Show he is a strong man who financially can support his new family.
D. Honor and respect the patriarch and matriarch of April's family.

If Donald does these things well, he will win April's family over and, more important than winning them over, he will help repair and restore the view they have of April. April's family will look at all that Donald does and give her credit for finally having good judgment in choosing a partner. So, it is important for Donald to understand the dynamics he is walking into.

The more information you have concerning your partner's parents, the more you are able to understand what it will take to win their support. If you take the attitude "I am not going to focus on anybody but my new partner" you take the chance of isolating yourself from the people who are important to them. I can assure you that when the honeymoon is over, in most cases, the extended family will have a huge influence on your blended family.

Returning to our diagram, there's still more to understand about the dynamics. What about April's brothers and sisters? They will respect Donald as long as April is happy. If he treats the children with kindness, then the siblings will for the most part be okay with him. However, these sisters and brothers may have developed a bond with April's ex's that can slow them down in receiving Donald into the family.

What about John's effect on the new blended family, the man April had a child with before she met Donald? You may think John has nothing to do with what is going on in Donald and April's house but that is not true. John has a huge reason to care about what goes on in their house because he has a daughter he is very much concerned about and he does not know Donald. It is John's responsibility to make sure his baby girl is loved, protected, and covered. (A real man will not leave that responsibility to anyone but himself to make sure his children are protected.) John and April may not have been able to make a go of it, but John is very interested in knowing who April is allowing to be around his daughter. By his very nature as a man, he will be skeptical of every man until he is sure his daughter is safe. Once John knows his daughter is safe from all harm, he will relax and allow Donald and April to run their home without interference for the most part.

April's brothers and sisters are very close to John. April and John were together for many years before they divorced. In the process of them being together, John has maintained a long relationship with April's family. Even though Donald is the new partner in the family, John is still a part of his child's life and that child is a part of April's larger family. April's parents are very close to John, seeing that he is the father of their first granddaughter, and they somewhat see him as one of their sons. Just because April and John ended their relationship, doesn't mean that John has ended his relationship with her family. It is important that Donald understands this relationship has nothing to do with him; it is the result of years of bonding together. If Donald wants to enter into the family and continue to move up the ranks, so to speak, he must not be insecure in his position as the new son-in-law. These are the real dynamics in a blended family and one has to be ready to deal with them to have a successful marriage.

When I met my wife, this was the case and I learned very quickly to warm up to the family without demanding they take me over my wife's ex-husband. My wife's ex-husband was someone who had been a part of my wife's family's life for over ten years. People who build authentic relationships cannot just turn them off as if the person never existed. If you try to demand the family gets rid of the ex by your unspoken demeanor, it will backfire and they will emotionally get rid of you. Yes April's family will respect her choice to marry Donald, but they will distance themselves from Donald and will not reinforce his new position in the family.

What should Donald do to bring stability to his relationship? The first thing Donald must understand is that if April wanted to be with her ex, John, the two of them would still be together. As a whole:

1. Donald must not be insecure as the new partner.
2. Donald must control his jealousy if any exists and place things in proper perspective.
3. Donald should not allow his emotions to get out of check, especially with anger. Remember the famous saying "never let them see you sweat."

It is imperative April is ready to assure Donald that John is a part of her child's life and there is nothing for him to worry about. April must be willing to show small steps of affection in the presence of John to make sure Donald is completely secure. When I mention small step of affection, I am suggesting holding hands, hugs, and speaking kindly with names of affection such as honey and sweetie.

Again, I mention John has been a part of April's family for the last ten years and that relationship is helpful to assure their daughter maintains a since of normalcy. April must over emphasize she is not interested in having a relationship with John even though she does have an invested interested in him being a part of his child's life. As a result, John must maintain a relationship with his child's family. (If this is your life scenario, this needs to be addressed before you get married, if possible. Don't make the mistake of not saying anything thinking that if nothing is said it means everything is okay. This conversation will come up and erupt in another form if you keep silent about it, thinking you don't have to address it.)

If Donald understands the family dynamics and continues to do everything with grace and love, he will win out as the new man in charge. The family will honor his position and John will give him the respect he deserves; John will take a back position. This may take a few years, so Donald must continue to be polite and full of patience as he seeks to be integrated into the family. Eventually he will change places in the hearts of the family without having to demand it.

The truth of the matter is the family wants April to be happy, and if she has chosen Donald for that assignment, they are pulling for Donald to win. Donald must not come into the family trying to make a statement and strong arm them to remove John from the family. That move on Donald part will be rejected by the family. Donald is new to the family; John is seen as family already. Plus John is the father of their first granddaughter; he will hold a special part in April's family. John will be always welcome as long as he continues to love his child. This is why it is important to study the dynamics of the family before you get involved.

Now there is a plus to John remaining a small part of the family. John has a neutral place to get to know Donald as a person who is going to be involved with his daughter. Donald should take the opportunity to show John he will be a good influence and bonus daddy for John's daughter. Donald will get a chance for John to see he is honorable and trust worthy. Every man wants to know the guy that will be around his children. This is especially true when the children are young between the age of six months and eighteen years old. For the most part, the ex has to trust the decision of the mother, however, whenever possible, they want to know the man for themselves. The grandparent's house is a good neutral ground for this to happen.

In my case, once the father knew I was a good man, his guard came down slowly and we were able to have non-threatening conversations. Please know this takes time and will not happen overnight. If you get into a boxing match, figuratively speaking, this will affect your relationship with your new partner. It will also hurt your ability to develop a good relationship with the extended family and the child. The family may see the problem being your insecurities and jealousy. Also, you will never win the battle of putting down a child's parent in the eyes of that child. The best thing you can do if you find yourself in Donald's position is to try and let John know you both have the same goal. Your goal is supporting John to have the best relationship humanly possible with his child. Let him know you are only there to be the bonus dad and will not try and move him out of the way, but fully support the mother's vision. When John sees Donald at the school program cheering his child on, when his child shows John what Donald brought her for her birthday, John will began to honor Donald's position. When you love another man's child, he will trust his child to your care and thank you for it.

Now, let's look at the dynamics of Larry in the family. This relationship of April's was a huge mistake. Larry is not a responsible man nor has he been a father to his son. April was the reason why the relationship did not work; she did not intend on taking care of a grown man. Larry and April never married, however, Larry is being asked to pay child support and he resents that his paycheck is being garnished. His child with April is in the middle of the discord.

How should Donald deal with his kind of tension? First, Donald must have great discipline and self-control in this matter. Larry's whole intention is to cause discord in April's life to get back at her for what he sees as an injustice done to him. Again, Donald has had to walk into what was already an intense situation that has nothing to do with him personally. Most men want to show their new partner they are there to protect them from belligerent behavior. If Donald begins to show aggression towards Larry, the testosterone match will be on. April might be happy she can hide behind Donald, but Donald will have created a new enemy to fight with, moreover the child will be distraught from all of the negative energy displayed by all parties involved. This is not the correct way to deal with the situation, and, if Donald was to choose this method, Larry will become a thorn in his and April's side for a long time to come.

There is a better way to handle this kind of difficult behavior. Donald has to keep his composure and not let his emotions get the best of him. Because Larry is not being reasonable and stepping up to take care of his parental responsibility, the only thing Donald can do is support April in her efforts. If Larry is at least spending time with his child, than Donald can began to establish a relationship with him as he picks up his child from April. April and Donald should pick up and drop off the child together at the beginning of their relationship. April should do the communicating while Donald just smiles and greets Larry with pleasantries. If Larry has a conscience, he will slowly begin to warm up to Donald.

Again, this is not an overnight process; it can take months if not a few years. While Donald is being a man of integrity, April may experience a heightened level of harassment or backlash. Larry most likely will believe since April has a new partner in her life he should not have to pay child support at all. He may feel that any money he gives to April will benefit Donald and Larry will highly resent it. As Donald slowly shows Larry that everything he gives is going to support his child, Larry will soften. Donald will now be in the house and will be supporting April and her children with his finances. As Donald gets a chance over a period time to show the money he has invested into Larry's child, Larry will be more inclined to pitch in. As the child becomes older, the child will demand more from his father and the child support hopefully will come without a fight.

Again, this is not an overnight fix; it will take time and a lot of patience. April should take the lead in the relationship with Larry, however, Donald can certainly be an adviser as to how she deals with him. Donald will do best if he keeps in mind the child is what is important, not his ego.

There is the situation that the biological father is not involved in his children's lives where it is common the mother will not see any support on a voluntary basis. If this was in April's case, she would have to take the failing party through the legal system to make him do the right thing. In a situation like this, the biological father will most likely not be a factor in the family dynamics, however the children will be affected from the loss of their parent.

You may ask the question, "Why would I want to go through all of this drama? I don't have anything to do with my new partner's old relationships." Here is the reality—anytime you marry someone with children it will affect your family with them in some way. This is the life of the blended family. If there are no children involved, then you are right, the old relationships should not be an issue. If your new partner wants to maintain a relationship with his or her ex, however, when no children are involved, I would question why and for what purposes.

When there are children, your new partner will have to deal with their father(s) and those men will want to know what is happening in your home because of their children. The truth of the matter is, although it is your house, they have a right to know what is going on with their child. Therefore, they will ask the children about you and if the report is not a favorable one, your new partner will be persecuted for your actions. If the children complain they are not happy with you, then the father of these children will come after you to protect his babies. When children do not get their way, they have a way of making you out to be the bad guy. You need an open relationship with everyone connected to the children so their parent will know you have the kids' best interest at hand.

You cannot say I am in love with my new partner and not deal with everything that comes with them. You cannot forsake the children and just deal with your new partner. This strategy will quickly go downhill. If you think you can do it, you will be a number added to the statistic of sixty percent of second marriages ending in divorce quickly. If you don't want to deal with these family dynamics, I highly suggest you marry someone who does not have kids. If you further want to escape such family dynamics, make sure you are child free as well. If you have children, all of what I have shared will apply to you. Before you say "I do," you need to know the dynamics of the family and what you will be dealing with. Don't go into this new relationship blind as if you are only going to be dealing with the woman alone.

The dynamics change as children become older. If you marry someone with adult children, then you do not have to deal with their fathers in most cases. The children can fight their own battles and you should not get involve with those relationships; simply give advice only when asked.

In short, the other dynamics you have with blending family are uncles, aunts, cousins, and the children's other siblings from their father's or mother's new partner. The strategy is still the same; use patience, get to know the other people, and build relationships. With my blended family, my bonus children's aunts, grandmother, or any of their extended family are all welcome to stay at my home when they come to town. These relationships have been building over the years and their father's sisters and mother accepted me as part of the family. They saw I loved the children as my own and they were endeared to me because of it. When people see you will love their cherished family member, they will receive you with open arms. It is not wise to have disagreements in front of the families you are trying to win over. Keep that in your home and away from the children. Everything you do in front of the children will be reported to their extended family because the children will tell it, good or bad. This will set you back in your effort to build healthy relationships with the families if you are arguing in front of the children.

I have dealt with the dynamics from Donald's point of view, however, what if April was coming into Donald family? The strategy is still the same; April must now win over Donald's family. The dynamics are a little different due to the fact that Donald's children in most cases are primarily with their mother. Donald's family may not be concerned with how April treats his kids, because Donald is a man and he is able to handle whatever problem may arise. Also woman are not likely to abuse a child when the father is very active in their lives. However, women have a tendency to want to be received by the family and are often disappointed when that family is slow to receive them. One of the reasons why they are slow to receive the woman has nothing to do with her. Some men have a tendency to bring short-term lady friends to family functions so when they bring in the new partner, the family will not invest energy into her until they know she will be around for a while. This feeling is often also projected toward the woman when the man has been married more than two times. The family has connected to the past relationships and does not want to have to deal with the emotional loss yet again. They most likely will hold back their affection until the new woman wins their hearts in time.

If you look at the dynamics of the family before you enter into the relationship, it will help you know how to deal with the issue that will arise. Remember, these issues take time, patience, and lots of love to navigate through. If you give love unconditionally, it will return back to you in time. It may feel like it never happens fast enough and you will have some major challenges along the way, but don't quit or revert to negative behavior because you will not win using these methods. Your goal is to build a healthy family and it will happen if you understand and do not react to the dynamics that happen in the family.

CHAPTER 5

Cinderella Syndrome

"A child's life is like a piece of paper on
which every person leaves a mark."
Author Unknown

I n a blended family, we must be careful not to show favoritism among the children—a practice I am totally against. We must guard against treating biological children well and bonus children unfairly. I call this the Cinderella Syndrome.

"Once upon a time there was a beautiful girl called Cinderella and she had two ugly step sisters who were very unkind and made her do all the hard work. She had to sweep the floors and do all the dishes while they dressed up in fine clothes and went to lots of parties." From ChildrenStory.com

In a blended family, this happens more often than you would believe. People often treat their bonus children like stepchildren in the story of Cinderella. They let their biological children get away with not doing the hard work and only assign the stepchildren to hard labor. This is horrible, cruel, and very un-loving. It may be done unintentionally, but you need to be aware of it and not fall into this behavior. Children will remember this kind of treatment and will resent you for what they deem as cruelty.

I want to share the things you must pay attention to so your bonus children will not feel hurt and abandoned by you. You need to focus on the children and what you owe them. Yes, you owe them! They did not ask to be here and since you made that decision for them, you owe them a safe place to grow so they can become productive citizens. The children did not ask to be a part of a blended family; you chose their parent and the kids are forced to be a part of the new marriage. In order for your home to be a place of love, there are a number of suggestions for you to consider.

First, you must accept all the children as if you gave birth to them. This is not a natural thing; this is something you must do intentionally. In our house, I had to close my eyes and picture my children asking in place of the bonus children. Often times my answer would change to a positive outcome when I pictured my children asking. If I saw my bonus children asking for special consideration, I may not have been as merciful to them. So close your eyes when your bonus children ask for something and see your children before you answer. If you really want to see if you are being fair, keep a log for three months and see what you have said yes to for your biological children and no to for your bonus children. You may be surprised at the results.

Also, if you buy one of the kids a treat, you must buy all of them a treat. I know the baby of the family gets perks, but in a blended family the kids do not understand this natural behavior of mom and dad and it will be misunderstood as showing favoritism. Be careful not to do this as it can breed resentment from the other children. Even if you do it secretly, the child will brag and tell the other kids about the special treat. I suggest if you do something for one in a blended family you do it for all. I know you will be tempted to lean towards your biological children, especially when your bonus children are being disrespectful. You have to hold back the urge, however, close your eyes, and be fair to all. If when your children are being disrespectful they are forgiven and blessed in spite of their behavior, you must treat your bonus children the same way.

As you accept all of the children as your own, do not call them your stepchildren. When you introduce them, call them your children. Don't ever use the words stepchildren when you introduce them. There is nothing more hurtful to a child or awkward for them than for you to make them feel as if they are an outsider to your friends and family. They are your children and part of the family, plain and simple. In a blended family there is no "step" in children. If you need to distinguish between them in front of people for various reasons, and only if it is necessary, call them your bonus children. The word bonus has a positive connotation and your children will feel as if you see them as a blessing and not a burden.

Now, this rule does not go both ways; the children are able to introduce you to their friends as stepmom or stepdad. Why? They will feel as if they are betraying their parents by giving you that title if their biological parent is very active in their lives. Remember, children are very loyal to their parents, in the good and the bad times. This is why it is a bad idea to speak negatively about the children's father or mother in front of them. You crush them beyond what you can ever imagine. Children idolize their parents and only want to hear great things about them. I know that parent may be a dead beat, but in the mind of that child their father or mother is pure gold. Allow them to see their parent for who they are as they grow up and formulate their own opinions. I know there are times you think you are helping the child to understand the kind of person they are dealing with, but allow them to find that out on their own. As much as you would like to, you can't stop them from being hurt when or if their parents disappoint them; this is life. In fact, this is part of their journey that will help them become great people in the future. When disappointment happens, and it will, just show them lots of love and attention. In your anger, however, do not talk badly about their father or mother as you would be only inflicting further pain on the child.

Again I am against forcing your bonus children to call you Mom or Dad because of their loyalty to their biological mother or father. The children did not have a choice in picking your new love and they should not be made to give them that title. I have counseled couples who felt this is unfair, but I don't think so at all. The children are caught in the divorce due to no fault of their own. They have lost their birth family and both parents are introducing new people into their lives. They are going through all kinds of sad emotions and are afraid of the unknown; we should not place any demands on them. The dynamics of their accepting their new reality is enough. They need lots of love, tender care, a lot of understanding, and a safe place to land. Allow them to call you by your name or anything that is respectful. However the title Mom or Dad belongs to the biological parent, until the children are ready to use that title for you.

If your partner only wants to deal with you and not your children, RUN as fast as you can. Please open your eyes. If he or she has children they are not dealing with now, let me say it again RUN. If a man or woman won't take care of the ones they brought into the world, they will not care for your children.

Men listen to this; if you are dealing with a woman who has a problem with you going to see your kids over at their mother's house, RUN! How can a woman ask a man to love her children and forsake his own? When a woman places these kinds of demands on you, she is not the woman you need to make a blended family with. It is your responsibility to love your children and give them a healthy environment to flourish into adulthood. You need someone who understands this, is willing to blend their lives into yours, and create a loving family together. Never put your children on the back burner! They must be first in your life and in the life of the new family. Children have the unique ability to bounce back and adapt to many things and situations. One thing that is very hard for them to bounce back from, if they ever, is rejection of love from a parent.

As you bring children together as one family, you must be very careful and watch their behavior closely. It is very uncomfortable to have some family conversations about sexuality. When kids are growing into teenagers, they are discovering things about their bodies. It is not wise to have boys and girls sleeping in the same bed or taking baths together once they are a certain age. When kids are in a blended family, they do not spend all of the time at your house, so it is important to make sure you talk with them about what is going on when they return from spending the night outside your home.

Also, look at the ages of the children they are hanging around with; if those kids are teens, it is likely that whatever music, video games, TV, and Internet they are involved in will be inappropriate for their young minds. This is one of the challenges of divorce; you don't get a chance to regulate what happens in the home of your ex. You need to cover your children in prayer, but watch as well as pray.

If your children don't want to go over to the ex's house, do some investigation into why. I am not telling you to be paranoid about it; I just want you to know you must watch and be alert about your children's behavior. With everything, keep a dialogue open and teach them to say something if something is wrong. Sexuality is real, as we all know, but many times we act as if it is not happening in our home; with kids this can be a mistake. Pay attention because they are receiving information from a lot of places that is affecting their minds. Keep the conversation open, even if it is uncomfortable.

As if blended families are not hard enough, let me add a few things you may not have thought about. What happens when your ex gets remarried and they have children with the other person and start a second family? Now your children have brothers and sisters from the other marriage. As time goes on, your children will become very close to their bonus brothers and sisters; you need to be ready to support those relationships. At some point in time, they are all going to want to spend time together as siblings at your house. It does not matter why you divorced your last partner, but the children should not suffer. This is where prayer, forgiveness, and maturity comes in. It may not be easy to welcome and accept these other children, however, these stepsiblings are a part of your children's lives and your children should be free to express their love with your full support. Whatever the reason your marriage failed, the children are innocent and should not be penalized for your ex's behavior. If you give forgiveness and accept these other children into your family, in the future it is more than likely that these children will honor you for your kindness. They will learn the truth when they get older and they will have high respect for you, knowing the sacrifice you made to include them.

You have to be careful not to place the Cinderella Syndrome on these other children because you have some unresolved issues with their parent. This is also true if infidelity happens in a marriage and a child is conceived. This is very hard to accept. The emotional pain and anger over what your partner did is real. I suggest you try to find out what is the root cause of the problem and try to save the marriage. However, if you stay in the marriage and commit to it, the child should not suffer for the act of the person who violated the vows. That child should be given the opportunity to know who his brothers and sisters are and should receive full support from all the parents involved. I have seen this situation in action and when forgiveness happens, the child is received and the family is healed in time. Over the years, I have seen this play out and when done with lots of prayer and forgiveness, the results are amazing. In some cases, I have seen where the marriage did not last, however, the child remains a part of the family because of the attachment of brothers and sisters. When people see your love is unconditional, they will honor you for a lifetime.

In a blended family, the ages of the children can make all of the difference. The older the children, the more challenging it will be to blend the family. If you meet your new partner when the child is an infant to four years old, you will be able to navigate through creating a blended family a little easier. If their biological parent is not in their life, the child will see you as their biological parent and will have no problem addressing you as such. Even if the biological parent is involved in his or her life, the child will still see it as normal family dynamics. If you enter the child's life between five and ten, they already have a routine in the house with their parent. This is a routine they probably enjoy because they have the full attention of the parent. Any change introduced into this routine will be contributed to the new partner's arrival. If the changes are to their benefit, they will give the biological parent the credit. If the changes take away some of their privileges, they will blame the new partner for the change.

I remember when I was single young man in my late twenties. I allowed my children to stay up as long as they wanted to; I did not believe they needed to be in bed early. We would stay up and watch TV all night or play video games. This was during their summer breaks when there was no school in the morning. My sons were at this time seven and nine years old. When I met my wife, she was in the health care profession. She would tell me that children needed their rest to grow. Her kids would go to bed around eight and nine o'clock. When we joined our families together, need I tell you what happened? I told my children they had to go to bed at nine o'clock and they blamed it on my wife. The truth of the matter is she shared the information with me, I read up on a few things, and it was my decision to give them the proper rest for their health. I made the decision, but my new partner was blamed for the action.

This is where children start formulating an opinion to like or dislike your new partner. You have to let them know it was your decision and your new partner had nothing to do with it. Even if they did make the choice, the children must believe the idea came from the biological parent. Here is another quick story; again my wife is a health conscious person so this went the other way in my favor with her children. My wife only purchased no sugar or low sugar cereal. Of course my children complained about the cereal being chosen for the family. So, I purchased, Fruit Loops, Frosted Flakes, and Lucky Charms, all while she was at work, to feed the kids. When she returned home, the kids were bouncing all off the walls and they voted from that day forward I would purchase the cereal. I must admit from that day forward, my food selection has been appreciated by all the children in the house, but despised by my wife. When it came to food, the children loved for me to take them out. I would take them to McDonalds and Pizza Hut and my poor wife just gave up. That's what happens in a blend family; you lose some and you win some.

When children reach the ages of eleven to sixteen, these are the most challenging years. If you come into your new partner's life when the children are this age, they will give you much attitude. This has nothing to do with anything or anybody; it's just youth and a lot of hormones running wild. Even in a traditional family with both parents in the home, at this age children are mouthy with attitude. Try to remember how you were as a teen and give them grace to get through this period. Children can be very defiant and manipulative at these ages, so don't take their actions personally. I read something on Facebook that said it all:

At 6 yrs "Mommy, I love you"

At 10 yrs "Mom, whatever"

At 16 "My Mom is so annoying"

At 18 "I wanna leave this house"

At 25 "Mom, you were right"

At 30 "I wanna go to Mom's house"

At 50 "I don't wanna lose my Mom"

At 70 "I would give up everything for my Mom to be here with me"

Remember, this is not a blended family issue; this is a life issue and how teenagers respond to everybody. If you hang in there, this will pass and the children will come around. From seventeen to eighteen, kids are trying to figure out where they are going to go to college and getting out of the house.

The last thing to cover is our grown children. I know what you are saying—we don't take care of adult children. That is true, however, they still need the support and love of their parents. When I do seminars on blending families, one of the things I hear often is adult children who feel they have lost their father or mother to the other person. It is as if, when a child turn eighteen years old, the commitment to parent them is over. The question is always asked, "How do I keep a relationship with my Mom or Dad when their partner is blocking me?" Too many time I have seen partners that are so anxious to get rid of the kids as if they are a threat to their relationship.

Many years ago, I experienced this same thing when my father and mother each remarried. I remember as a young man feeling isolated from my parents because their mates did not welcome me into their homes. Yes, I could go over to my parents' houses, but there was no relationship being nurtured. I was made to feel unwanted, not loved, and "how long are you going to be here?" If I needed something, it was not given to me openly by my parents but secretly so their mates would not find out. I lost my parents to their mates and it was a huge awaking. I felt as if I was on my own. This went on for many years. I am glad to report our relationships were restored and now I am very close to my mother. May I add my mother added two new family members a brother and sister whom we love deeply. My dad returned back home after he divorced his wife and remained a great father until his death. However, for a few years, in my eyes my parents were missing in action. This is why you must choose your partner wisely. They can have an impact on the lives of your children forever, positive or negative.

You must know your children will judge you for your actions. I am ministering to a family right now whose mother is sick and none of the adult children will take care of her. After getting to know the family, I asked the question how was their childhood? It came to light that the mother had been busy running the street after new men and not investing into her children. Now she is paying the price of being sick with no support from the family she neglected. You can put your children on the back burner but when you need them, they may put you on the back burner. The only people you can depend on is your family. Your children are small today, but one day they will grow up to become adults and they will remember the investment you made into their lives. If you are stopping someone's adult children from spending time with their parent, I caution you to stop. Allow your adult children into your home and make them feel welcome as they may be the ones who end up taking care of you.

"Once upon a time there was a beautiful girl called Cinderella and she had two ugly step sisters who were very unkind who made her do all the hard work. She had to sweep the floors, do all the dishes, while they dressed up in fine clothes and went to lots of parties."

You do know how the story ended; Cinderella ended up in a palace without the people who mistreated her!

CHAPTER 6

Joining the Family Together

"May your joining together bring you
more joy than you can imagine.
Congratulations on your engagement!"
Author Unknown

Now that you know a little more about what you have to deal with to make a blended family work, do you still want to go forward with becoming one? If you are not sure you are ready to jump in completely, keep looking for the right situation where you would be willing to give 100%. While dating and trying to find a life partner, I strongly recommend you do not introduce your children to your significant other until you are 100% sure they are the one you are going to marry. In my strong opinion, it is a huge mistake to introduce your children to a temporary relationship. You should never bring different people into the lives of your children only to find out that the relationship did not work a short time later. Children can become attached to new people in a very short time.

In this day and time, living together without marriage has become the norm. I highly suggest you do not model this behavior in front of your children. If you are single and you decide to live with someone, it should only involve you so no children are hurt. When you have children, they should be your greatest concern; living with someone without marriage should not be an option. It is unfair to get your children attached and have them trust a person only to remove them out of their lives when the relationship does not work. In order to avoid this, it's very simple; just don't introduce them to your children until you know they are the person you are going to spend the rest of your life with.

As I said, children will become very attached to people who show them love and affection. I am speaking about smaller children from the age of three to around six years old. When you break up with a person your child had become attached to, your child will feel the loss as well. After ending a relationship, most people will meet new people to continue to find their soul mate. You cannot expect the children's emotions to switch like yours to a new person you are introducing. The example you are giving your children is not a healthy one. Again, this is the reason I suggest you do not introduce your children to new relationships that will not become permanent. If you do this, when you introduce your children to the one" you are going to marry, they may feel a bit of hesitation not knowing if the person will be around long term, especially if they may still be feeling the loss of the last person they were attached too.

If the child is eight to twelve years old, they are developing their own personality and may not bond with the next person you introduce them to. You want to be careful not to judge or demand the child treat your new relationship as family if there is no marriage. The child may not feel safe in investing their emotions into someone that may not be around. Again, if you have been dating a few people over the life of the child, your new partner must be patient with winning the child over.

From the age of thirteen to seventeen years old, the child is a teenager who most likely feels no one knows what they are talking about. These years are very challenging even if the children are your own. If you are marrying someone with teenagers, you will have a hill to climb, however, following my suggestions you will get through it. You need to have lots of love and patience towards your bonus children. If you pull the card "I am the man/woman around this house and you will do what I say" without building a relationship, you will cause damage you do not want in the relationship with the child. At this moment of building a family, do not used the Lion Mentality of Take Over.

The Lion Mentality of Take Over goes something like this: when a lion comes into a new pride, he fights all of the other lions to show he is the new king of the pack. He fights the father of the baby lions, he jumps on the teenage male lions and, in some cases, demands they leave and go live somewhere else. He has been known to kill the baby lions.

If you employ the Lion Mentality of Take Over as you create a blended family and try to assert yourself as the new king or queen of the house, you will have less than desirable results. If you do this, the relationship with your bonus children will be built on a lot of resentment and not on love. The way you join your family together will have profound effects on your blended family for years to come. You can set your family going in the right direction or you can place it on course for disaster. This can make your children not value the family relationships in the future and, when they become adults, repeat the same cycle that was modeled for them.

The person you should be looking to be with is someone who loves your children and you. They are excited about your dreams and want to support your visions. They love themselves and their family; they speak highly of their parents. When you go out to eat, they are kind to the wait staff and are respectful to all they meet.

When you decide you have found your new lifetime partner, it is time to begin the process of blending the families together. This can be a lot of fun and will give your partner the opportunity to get to know your children. You should start planning a variety of things to do as a family. These outings should be fun things the kids will enjoy so they will look forward to having these moments with your new partner. Little kids get very excited and want to be the center of attention, so give them time to shine without raining on their parade. Kids are anointed to play, they are born to play, and to make them sit down for long periods of time is not natural for a child, especially between the ages of three and eight. If you have teenagers, no matter what you plan, they most likely are not going to fully cooperate. Most teens are very self-centered and only think about what's in it for them.

When you introduce your new partner to your children, don't be overly concerned about the kids being on their best behavior. I know you want your partner to believe that he/ she is not getting ready to adopt bad or misbehaved children. I suggest before you introduce your new partner to your kids, give your partner a run down on how they may respond so there will be no surprises. For example, tell them that your child, Jayson, is very active and all over the place. Tell them Sharon is going to talk your ears off. Make sure your partner is prepared for the encounter. Don't pressure the kids to conform; prepare the adult to receive.

When I met my wife, her children had two different personalities. The young one wanted me to play soccer with him the very first time he met me. He was heavy into sports; I could win him over if I loved what he loved. So, I began to play soccer with him. That was his way of connecting with me.

My bonus daughter was around seven years old and could understand her mom and dad had just separated. She was not ready to open up to a new person. My wife's daughter was loyal to her father and was not moved by my presence in the beginning. I had to be kind and nice. As long as I did not ask her to break her loyalty to her father in any way, she was fine. As time went on and she saw I was going to be a part of her life, she began to give me room to "rent" in her heart. Notice what I said: I was given a place to "rent" in her heart. I had not invested enough into her life for me to own a part of her heart; as of yet it was rented space only. If I didn't continue to deposit love, I would be evicted from the little space I had been given. This is why I said the older the children are, the harder it is to win them over. You can do it, however, it just takes a lot of time and love.

My suggestion to win over the children is to begin to do things they enjoy. When you and your new partner are going out by yourselves, then you can do what you like to do. As you blend the families together, however, do what the children like to do as this will go a long way. You have to invest in the children and court them as well.

Now, if you're new partner has children, cross your fingers that the kids hit it off together. Children will let down their guard towards each other much faster than they will to a new adult in their life. If the children are close in age, this will help. If they are not close in age, the older children may not give the younger kids much of their time. It will take them a little longer to warm up to the younger ones. The younger ones will look up to the older children if they are kind to them. Again, have these conversations with your children and inform them of what to expect. This will help them support the new person you have fallen in love with.

Whenever you leave to return back to your respective places, ask your children what they liked or disliked about the experience. You know your children so discern between what is a natural fear of the new relationship and what is a legitimate concern. If your children had a fun time, they will want to go back again. Why? Because children are anointed to play.

At the beginning, as you are blending families together, the key is play, play, play. When you need to be serious or deal with homework or school, don't do it in this early, fun-focused environment. Retreat to your own places and deal with these issues singularly as the biological parent. When it comes to any kind of discipline towards housework or homework, each parent should deal with their own children. Remember, your partner is renting space in your children's hearts and has not purchased the right to correct them as of yet.

While you and your partner are dating and blending the family together, it should be about fun, fun, and more fun. Now, children will always complain about things they have never done before, so don't listen to them when you come up with exciting things for them to do. Kids will keep doing the same things over and over again, so it is our job to expose them to new and exciting adventures. Some of those things should be educational as well, such as trips to Washington DC and New York City, visiting local museums, and doing fun science experiments, etc. The more you expose your children to the more likely you may be to discover they are gifted in some of these areas. My bonus son ended up going to school on a baseball scholarship, my nephew is becoming a professional bowler, and one of my nephews is now an entertainer at Disney. When you do a variety of things, kids will find more opportunities to grow into something special.

Let's say that everything is a green light go and the family is gelling with only a few minor challenges. Now that you have decided to move forward with making this a blended family, I think it is important to do a wedding ceremony joining the two families together. My wife and I did not do this and we regret it till this day. Our children have said Eunice and I robbed them of participating in that special time in our lives. We went into the pastor's office solo to make our marriage official. No children, family, or friends got to share in our special moment. It was both our second marriage and we didn't want to make a huge deal about it. That was a mistake on our part. Marriage is a big deal and should be treated as such. When we got married many years ago, I did not think our children would have participated willingly. I have since learned my daughter would have participated and she isn't happy we did not give her that option. Children will go kicking and screaming but in the end they will be glad you asked them to be a part of your special moment.

Here is what you should do to make the wedding a great moment for the whole family. I am not saying it should be big or an expensive event, but your children should have a part in your special day. They need to know you pledge your allegiance to the entire family. They need to see you make those vows and honor them to the best of your ability.

I suggest you make an opening confession to love the children and honor them as your own. If you have spent quality time winning them over during the course of the year, they will have warmed up to you and should be glad to be an added part of the wedding. Children love to be the center of attention and they will get a big kick out of the day, dressing up, taking pictures, and being told to smile. I am telling you up front they will sometimes act as if they don't want to be included, but they really do. Each one of us knows our own children; try and get them to participate in a few pictures so they will be able to look back at the day with fond memories.

If you can afford it, take the whole family on a weekend celebration. You know what to do for this time together—FUN, FUN, and MORE FUN! I know from my counseling work that most men leave the children with their ex-partner. I recommend you include them in the entire celebration so they will feel a part of the new family. After you celebrate with them, then you and your new partner can have your honeymoon time alone.

Here is another very important point I suggest you consider. You and your new partner should move into a totally new house if possible. This is a huge deal—more than you can imagine—and will place both families on equal footing. Let's say, for instance, you move into the man's house and he has two girls. It is a three bedroom house and he has the master suite while his daughters each have one room. When you move in with your sons, your partner's children have already claimed their territory in "their" house. Even though you have joined two families into one, you still have moved into "their" house. The children will let the bonus children know they are in "their" room. When you move into your partner's house, it may be very hard to feel as if it is your house together. It might be difficult for your children to connect to this home also. In any times of conflict, your bonus children will make sure your biological children know that they are a visitor. If you and your new spouse move into a new place from day one, this will not be an issue as everyone would join together on new territory. The house will be "our" house and not "their" house.

The same line of thinking applies to the adults. If a man moves into a woman's house, when something needs to be fixed, he will look to her to pay for it because it is "her" house. The man will not take ownership in the home because he is moving into "her" house and not "our" house. When disagreement happens, and it will, the "get out of my house" card may be played. Sometimes children in their tantrums use the phrase "get out of MY room." I hear this same underlying problem all of the time when I consult married couples. Whoever moves in will be threatened with the famous words, "This is MY house." The children will also use this phrase whenever they are upset with their new brothers or sisters. In order to avoid these conversations, a new home needs to be rented or purchased before you get married if possible.

When you move into a new home, it becomes everybody's house and this will eliminate the problem. Do not put your biological kids who live in the house full time in the bedrooms and the bonus kids who come over on the weekends in the basement or on the couch. Give each child equal space even though they don't have equal time in the house. I understand this may not be possible because of the budget and/or the size of the house. If this is the case, please have a discussion with your partner and children about these dynamics. Children sometimes see this as unfair treatment if they are made to sleep on the floor while the other kids sleep in the bed. Make new sleeping arrangements to accommodate all of the children.

After the wedding celebration, you need to create new traditions for your new blended family. If you have old traditions you celebrated before you were married, you should keep them. If your old traditions isolate a part of your new family, however, then you should change them to include everyone. I do believe in some cases you'll have to make room for the ex-spouses to continue their own traditions as well. I remember when I first met my wife, her children's father came over on Christmas morning to open up gifts with his children. This was their family Christmas tradition. (I feel the children should not suffer just because their parents did not remain together. They have suffered enough from the divorce.) I remember the first few Christmases I would wait until they opened their gifts with their dad before I came over. Their dad needed to bond with his children and they needed their mom there to enjoy the moment. I understand children need to have special time with both parents without outside influences. The first few years, this arrangement may have been uncomfortable for all who were involve, however, because we faced the challenge head on to the credit of all of us, we rose to the occasion for the sake of the children.

It is important for you and your new partner to create new traditions for your family. We did in our blended family and it has turned out to be so much fun. One of the things we did every summer was go on a vacation as a family. This is one of the greatest memories our children have and talk about even today. One summer we drove a conversion van from Cleveland, Ohio to Las Vegas, Nevada, over 4,000 miles round trip. The best times in my life where when I spent them with family. My wife and I were in our early thirties then and we didn't have a lot of money, just had a lot of love for each other. We made it to Las Vegas and during this time Vegas was very kid friendly. They had amusement parks and roller coasters at most of the hotels. We played and had so much fun the kids always wanted to go back for vacation. In fact, Las Vegas is still one of their favorite places to go. Do you know why? We took them there and they feel happy in this city because it reminds them of the fun times they had as children.

One year I had a small 4-door 1980 Toyota Corolla hatchback. We took the children from Cleveland, Ohio to Orlando, Florida to go to Disney World. They fussed and complained all the way, however, today they talk about that trip as well as how much fun they had. In order for us to afford to get into the parks, we had to do a few timeshare presentations to get some free tickets. My children remember those presentations as fun times even though when we were doing them they said they hated it. They had a fit we had to spend our morning listening to something we were not going to buy. However, today they just remember the fun they had at the parks and the love we showed them having a good time. If you spend time investing into your blended family, it will pay off big time. Love a lot, laugh a lot, and play a lot. To capture those fun moment and new traditions, I purchased a DVD video camera. I wanted to create home movies of our trips so I could capture the children having fun. Those trips were in the early 90s and we watch those videos even today with much joy. When I purchased the camera, the kids would say "please stop filming us," but I didn't listen to them; today all of them say "thank you." They are glad I kept videoing them so they would have something to look back on and remember the good times. Here's my point as you create new traditions—you can't listen to children when they say they are not having fun because children complain about everything. As long as you know they are having a great experience, keep creating new, long-term memories that will change their lives.

I have counseled many people who want this change to be overnight. It does not happen that way; it takes a lot of time. Even today, after what I consider success, we are still dealing with challenges in our blended family. After doing the best you can—and in some cases that is a darn good job—children can see things a different way. I encourage you to keep on showing love and hopefully the kids will come around.

It took a long time for our children to trust the person we choose to be our partner. Remember, I told you boys love their mother and young men are very protective of their mother. Men, if you threaten or harm their mother in any way, you will never gain the respect of her sons. Ladies, if you treat the man disrespectfully, he will soon leave the relationship. He may be there in body, but his heart and mind will be long gone. A man needs to feel respected in his home by the woman who stands by his side. If you build him up by your words and actions, you will be building up a solid foundation in your own home.

As you bring your new family together, enjoy the journey, love your partner, love the children, and enjoy your life. There will be challenges with your blended family just as there are challenges with traditional families. In a blended family, your bonus children will be one of the biggest challenges, however, if you give those children unconditional love, they can be one of your biggest joys. Keep loving and keep going; this is a lifetime commitment that will reap lifetime benefits in the end.

CHAPTER 7

Who Should Discipline
in the New Family

"Many parents are finding out that a pat on the
back helps develop character if given often enough,
early enough, and low enough."
Author Unknown

This is one of the most important issues in a blending family. Who should discipline when the kids get out of line? In a traditional family, the issue is not who, but how the parents should discipline. In a blended family, it is all about who should discipline. This is the number one complaint I receive when counseling blended families— the children are disrespectful and the bonus parent does not feel like it is dealt with properly. According to the bonus parent, the biological parent allows the children to get away with way too much. The truth of the matter is most parents show mercy to their own children and some people are far too eager to come down hard on their bonus children. Keep in mind, we may never agree with the way others raise their children; we all do things differently.

Let me say on the front end, I know there has been a huge debate on spanking children. I am not a doctor who practices child psychology, so I will leave that up to the experts. When I was growing up, we received spankings in school by the principal. If we were disobedient outside, our neighbors spanked us and then our mothers and fathers took over when we got home. I want to say this as loud as I can—those days are gone! You will go to jail if you assault a child. You may call it discipline but the law calls it assault; this is the day and time we live in. Hitting your children could have very negative consequences.

Watch out for another way of abusing children—cursing them out like you are speaking to someone in the street. This is emotional abuse at its highest which will destroy your children's self-esteem and confidence. I don't believe speaking to a child this way is discipline at all. Just because your parents did it to you does not make it a standard for you to do to your children. I hope if you are using abusive methods you will break the cycle of violence and seek new ways to discipline your children.

In a blended family, the biological parent should take the lead in disciplining his or her own children. The partner should take a back seat of support only. When I first got married, I did not do this and it almost destroyed my family. I felt my wife was too soft on her children. The way I saw it, she needed my help to pull them in line. When she would ask them to do something, they would give her a lot of back talk. I grew up in an era that when your mother said jump you said "how high?" I perceived that when children talk back to their parents, it is a sure indication they are being disrespectful. In my house growing up, a child was not given a voice to express themselves or debate.

Now on the other hand, my wife wanted and encouraged the dialogue. My wife had been running her home this way long before I came into her life. My wife does not believe in spanking at all. When she wanted to get a point across, she discussed it with her children. She believed if the kids could openly express themselves they would be able to learn how to communicate with anybody as they became adults. As I witnessed, both mom and child would be very intense in their expressions and dialogue. I didn't like it and felt she needed my help to put those over-talking, disrespectful kids in their place. I knew just how to do it; get me a belt! Let me tell you this was the wrong move on every level.

This is wrong for many, many reasons. The first and foremost reason is I was taking the position I was right and my wife was wrong. Who told me that my way is the right way? My truth is my truth, but it may not be the ultimate truth. If you ever go into a conversation thinking you have the ultimate truth, it is not a conversation; you are demanding a person follow your instructions. Whenever you are having a discussion, you must leave room for the idea you may not be right in how you are viewing the issue. The very fact you leave a door open will cause you to listen to the other person's ideas or suggestions. Once you have all of the information together, then you can make an educated decision. I had set in my mind that my wife did not know how to handle her children and that my way was better. This is the wrong way to communicate with your partner and it will not give you positive results. No one likes a know it all; it is a huge turn off to anybody.

Here is the second reason against disciplining someone else's children. Whenever you are disciplining someone else's child you need to remember that the child is not your own flesh and blood. If you are a spanker, for instance, you will have a tendency to spank them too hard and too long. This is not the first time the child has probably done something wrong. You will go back and spank them for all of the things they have done in the past and you'll want to prove a point that you are in charge. Therefore, you'll have a tendency to not be merciful in your corporal punishment.

Since you want to make sure you send a message to the child, you will not be kind in your discipline to them.

If you, by intention or by mistake, put a mark on that child as a result of your punishment, you will be in trouble with the law. When the child goes to school, church, or day care, by law that institution must call the authorities and report it as abuse. They will immediately remove the child from the house and you will be arrested. The second outcome could really escalate—the child will tell their real father or mother about what you did. That parent will come over to your house and it will not be a pretty altercation. It does not matter what the child did wrong, your putting your hands on them will supersede all and any matters. When the biological parent comes, they will be ready to meet the challenge. This may escalate very quickly out of control. Remember how I talked about establishing an amicable relationship with the children's biological father or mother? If you hurt their child, this goes right out the window. Now the father or mother is talking about pressing charges or doing harm to you. Do not forget about the grandparents, uncles, and aunts who could turn against you. If you hurt a person's child, you will see the bear come out of them and it is hard to repair the relationship after that. In order to avoid this, keep your hands off of your partner's children.

The third thing that will happen concerns the space you are renting in you bonus children's hearts. You have not earned the right to purchase a part in their heart yet. That purchase normally does not happen until they look back and realize the sacrifices you've made to love them and their parent. If you discipline them, they quickly will evict you out of their heart and all of the work you have been doing will have to be rebuilt. Children will forgive their parents for almost anything. If parents spank their own child, that child tomorrow will forgive their father or mother. You, however, will not get the same treatment. They will hold it against you and will blame their biological parent for allowing it to happen. These things will not turn out well and should be avoided at all costs.

There is a way to discipline the children so all involved will be on the same page. You have to understand most parents will give their own children much grace; however they may not be as easy on their bonus children. This may not be intentional or on purpose; we just give mercy to ourselves and our own and are usually harder on others. You see your children as your seed, a part of you, and your heart is connected to them. This is the reason that each parent should discipline their own child.

So how do you discipline children in a blended family? The discipline must come from the biological parent. The biological parents must give the request or demand to the child, such as when a child has to do chores in the house or go to bed on time, etc. After the order is given, the bonus dad/mom can support that order by reinforcing what the biological parent has said. For example, consider the boy who is told by his biological father not to play video games during the week because of the need to study for school. The dad works during the evening shift while the bonus mother is at home. The son comes home from school and starts playing video games one day. His bonus mom should say, "Your father said you are not allowed to play video games doing the week." She must say "your father said." This way she is not giving the directive; she is supporting what the child's father told him. That child cannot argue with his bonus mom about the rule. He has to take it up with his biological father when he gets home from work.

If the bonus mom gives the directive, depending on the age of the child, she may hear these famous words "You are not my mother." Now she'd have to react to the son being defiant, which could turn ugly. This is why the directive must come from the biological parent. However, because the directive came from the child's father, she gets the chance to put the weight on him to deal with his son. When the father gets home, he must address his son's action and administer the appropriate punishment. The son cannot be angry with his bonus mother because she never requested anything of the son; she just supported what the father said. If the bonus mother had given the directive, the son would blame her which will began to build a negative relationship between them. This is what you want to avoid in a blended family at all costs. The biological parent must give the order of discipline or it may cause problems in your family.

One of the things appropriate for the son to do is apologize to his bonus mother. It is very important the son hears from his father that his defiance toward her will not be tolerated. If the father allows this to go unaddressed, the son will get the message that what his bonus mother says doesn't matter and he will handle her disrespectfully every time. This is inappropriate behavior that must be curbed.

Let's look at another example. In this case, the biological mother tells her daughter she is not allowed to be on the phone after 7:00 pm. Now the mom is at work and the bonus dad is at home watching the children. The way for him to build a relationship with the daughter is to communicate that her time is coming to a close and she should get off of the phone as "her mother said." The bonus father shouldn't wait until 7:00 pm then demand the girl hang up phone. He should let her know she has ten minutes left to bring her conversation to a close. When 7:00 pm arrives, the daughter should not have a problem hanging up the phone. If she refuses to hang up the phone, then the mother must discipline her for being disrespectful. If the biological parent does not deal with the child's disrespect, the child will not honor their bonus parent.

What happens if the biological parent is allowing an activity the bonus parent strongly disagrees with? How should it be handled? You should never, never, ever discuss this disagreement in front of the children. The children may use this division to drive a wedge between you and your mate. Instead, you and your mate should go into another room and come to an agreement you both can live with. Each person should give the best reason why they see it the way they do and what they think is the possible outcome. After coming to an agreement, with a united front, the parents should share the decision with the child. Again, the biological parent should give the directive to their child. There will be many things you will disagree upon, however, try to always have a united front. If the children feel the bonus parent is behind the directive, it could possibly cause a problem.

There was time in our home when our children would call their other biological parent and complain about the decision we made. Consider allowing your children to do this as long as it is in the best interest of the child. You may find your decision will hold up in most cases, supported by your ex. Let say, for instance, my fifteen year old bonus daughter wanted to go to an un chaperoned party of high school seniors. It is a situation my wife and I are not comfortable with. If she calls her biological father saying her mother is being unfair, it is reasonable to think he will agree with our decision because he has his daughter's best interest at hand. I know there will be times when the other parent will disagree with your decision. In these times, because you know all of the information, you ultimately will have to do what is best for your child.

I was once counseling a couple struggling with this issue of discipline. The bonus dad had been in the navy for a few years. When he returned home, the bonus son was seventeen years old and not willing to follow the rules of the house. His mother would ask him to be home at a certain time and the son would not listen. He was asked to be in at 10:00 pm but he would come home about 3:00 am or sometimes not at all. The bonus dad wanted to deal with the son man to man. I suggested, however, it would not be the right thing to do. It was his mother's responsibility to take disciplinary action.

You may ask how they got to the point where the son did not respect his mother. It turned out when her children were younger, the mother would administer discipline but not follow through and, as a result, the children received mixed messages. The son learned as a kid when his mother said something she didn't really mean it. The situation came to a head when her husband returned home. In his eyes, he saw his wife being taken advantage of, something he wanted to correct. Now, the children do not want their world altered because they have learned how to manipulate the situation and have it set so it is working for them. They know how to work their mother's heart and get their demands met.

The mom did want things to change; she had lost control of her family and she welcomed the help of her husband now that he was home. I suggested the mother show her displeasure with her son for his continual defiance of her demands. I also suggested the bonus dad stay close around so if her son decided to challenge his mother he would be ready to step in to bring order. I made it clear the bonus dad was not to order the discipline; he was there to be fully supportive of his wife.

The son was back to his routine and failing to obey his curfew. The discipline I suggested was for his mother to go into his room and take back everything she had purchased; all his clothes, shoes, sheets from the bed, TV, video games— everything. Just leave him with the underwear he was wearing. I told her to place it all in her room so when he returned home she would have his full attention. She could do all this because she knew she had the backing of her husband and could be confident her son would back down. Consequently, the son came home very upset to find his belongings missing and to learn his mother had taken a stand.

This is where understanding the dynamics of the family and how getting support from all sides is important. The bonus dad did not say a word; he was just there as support. If he had addressed the son, in the boy's anger, the situation could have gone the wrong way. After everything was said and done, the young man apologized to his mom and promised he would not behave that way any longer. He also apologized to the bonus dad who could now share his own experience of running the streets at night and impart wisdom into the young man's life. This family handled the situation the right way. Now the young man is doing the right thing and the family is moving in the right direction. They also had two younger sons who were watching to see the outcome and they have also continued to stay on the right road.

Let me share another technique that will help you in this area of discipline. My wife and I would play good cop, bad cop to our children. Let's say our kids wanted to play video games during the week and the rules were absolutely not. I would go to bat on behalf of the children and say to their mom, "Let them do it just today." Through this method, I was able to gain brownie points with the children. My wife and I did this with things that were not major issues and they were things we talked about ahead of time. When my sons wanted to stay up past their bed time, I would tell them to go to bed and my wife would say. "Let them stay up for another hour." My sons would make me laugh when they said, "Yes, Dad, listen to your wife." What we learned was the kids enjoyed us being an advocate for their needs. Doing this will help you win them over and give you more space to rent in their hearts. Don't always be against the things the children want to do; you will never win their hearts opposing them all of the time.

Children are people pleasers. They love to get stickers and praise for their actions. As the bonus parent, keep reinforcing the positive and leave the discipline to the biological parent. Go behind closed doors and hammer out the issues between your mate, then come out of the room with a united front. Your children will take their cue from you. If you send them mixed messages, they will use them to divide and conquer. Work together and do it with a lot of love and patience. The old saying is true, people don't care how much you know until they know you care. Children don't care about what you say until you show them how much you love them.

I was counseling a couple who had a thirteen year old son who would not speak to the bonus dad when he

The Making of a Blended Family

walked into the room. The bonus dad took the attitude "if he doesn't speak to me, I am not going to speak to him." You can see how he was approaching the situation totally wrong. First of all, the bonus dad is the adult and the thirteen year old is the child. It is the adult's job to win over the child and get him to open up. I began to explain to the father that he had to do something enjoyable with the child, like take him to a basketball game, ride a bike with him, or play a video game with him. (All young men love video games.) The dad was looking for this thirteen year old to meet him on his level when he should have come down to the level of the thirteen year old. This father had not been willing to do the work necessary to rent space in the boy's heart.

Because the son would not speak to him, the bonus dad said the son was the cause of their marital problems. Do you want to know where this relationship ended up—that's right, divorce! In most cases, a bonus parent will not win this battle over a mother's child. If you are not willing to invest the time into the lives of your bonus children, then you need to marry someone without children. Also, if you won't love your bonus children, don't expect someone to invest in loving the children you bring into the relationship. If a person will not honor your children, tell them to keep on stepping and move on because they are not the one for you. If you love your bonus children and leave the discipline to their biological parents, you will win their hearts. When you win the children's hearts, your mate's heart will soon follow.

CHAPTER 8

Family Events and Gatherings

The things you say out of anger do not come with a return policy.
Watch what you say.
Author Unknown

There are a lot of challenging moments for blended families. Family events can be some of the most challenging times. When it is time for family functions, such as graduation, school programs, children's sports activities, etc., you will discover everyone is involved. It is important you remember the children in these moments and leave all of the drama for another time. You might be tempted to make a point to the other side to show you are upset with decisions that have been made in the past, however, during the children's event is not the time to do it.

First of all, you are in the children's environment; they are trying to make the best impression with their peers. If you need to make a point, something could be said that may get out of hand. The embarrassment you will cause the children could be devastating for them. They will never live this moment down in front of their friends, how their mom's or dad's partner acted in such an inappropriate way at a school event. If there is negative tension in any way, it will ruin the evening for the child who is only looking for approval from his parents so that he can grow in confidence to take on the world. We owe our children to be on our best behavior so they will be able to lift their heads high and be proud of the entire family. Therefore, at any function or event, it is imperative you be on your best behavior. Later on in the course of our blended family, I was blessed to have my ex-wife's extended family be very supportive of me whenever we attended an event. They are people of class and once I proved my love to their niece and nephew, I was embraced fully.

Here are a few events I attended and how I handled them. My younger son played hockey at a young age. My wife wanted me to go to every game to support him and be with her. This was very early on in our relationship; she did not know how to work the video camera and wanted to capture these memories. My bonus son's biological father was very involved in his life and wanted to be there to support his son. Just because my wife and her ex did not make it as a married couple does not mean their son should not have both of their full support. The child should not have to choose one parent over another and I as the new partner should not place that demand on the child or my wife.

It is absolutely unacceptable behavior to prohibit the children's family members on either side from attending events important to the children! Never should it be said, "If your dad is coming then your mother can not be there" or "If your mom and I come, your dad is not allow to be there." Children have the right to enjoy their childhood without the drama of adult relationships hovering over them.

Now, if my wife was in fear of her ex-husband because he was an abusive man, then I would have her deal with those issues legally with my support. However, it is not my place to put limiting demands like those above on my new relationship because I am having insecurity issues. In a blended family, you have to learn how to get along at these events. Children should be able to have both parents and extended relatives at all functions.

My wife and I made a conscious decision to make sure the children's dad (her ex) and the children's mom (my ex) would be welcome in our home and at events for the sake of the children. We worked very hard to make this happen and I can truly say that over twenty-six years we never had a fallout in front of the children. As young children, our combined kids were blessed to enjoy their biological parents without unnecessary negativity and drama.

When my bonus son had hockey games, I would attend along with my wife's ex, his dad. At first, this was not a comfortable or pleasant time for any of us. It was something we had to make a conscious effort to work through. When we would get to the game, we would sit on one side of the rink and my wife's ex would sit on the other side. This was in the early part of our relationship with each other. I did not know her ex and he did not know me. We all had a common interest, however, which was the well-being of the child. I learned very early when we all got together that my bonus son would lean in favor of his biological dad so I did not try to be his dad's equal during these moments. I would step back and just play a supporting role to his mother and be a fan of my bonus son as he played the game in front of his dad. When his dad was around, I did not try to upstage his father and try to get my bonus son to show me any kind of affection. For me to require or suggest that could make him feel disloyal to his dad and also give his father more reason to be offended at my actions. When he was around his dad, it was father and son time; I was there to do a job for his mother—video record the memories. You, as the new partner, have to be ok with this. This is the child's moment and your role is to support the child and give him the opportunity to bond with his parents. You can create opportunities to bond with the child when his dad is not around because you are living in the house with the child.

After the game was over, my son would always run to his dad for approval and my wife would run over to her son to congratulate him on a great game. So it would not appear I was being standoffish, I would slowly meet her over there and say my hellos to my son and his father. At first, I was not overzealous. I would just say hello and I look at my bonus son and say great game. If I needed to be the first to speak hello, I would. I never wanted to get into any altercation. My wife's ex loved his son and had every right to be there to support him.

Each time there was a game, this process became easier and easier because we always kept our children's best interest at hand. Before long, after a few years had passed, we would find ourselves sitting on the same side of the rink. There always remained a bit of caution but our guards slowly came down. I eventually began to ask him about his day and we started the journey of becoming joint parents to his children.

You may take the stand that you should just stay home and not go to these events. Doing this would rob the child of the relationship you are trying to build. Children want their parents to come and support them at events. Would you stay home if your biological son was playing sports? You need to realize these are your bonus children; if you are trying to break down the walls, you must treat them as if they are your biological children. Were there days I did not want to deal with the emotions that it took to rise above all of it? Absolutely. I wanted the best family I could have, however; I knew what I signed up for and that it would take a lot of effort.

I remember when my wife's ex brought his new partner to the game with him. My wife had an opportunity to appreciate the level of commitment it takes to keep a smile on your face in an awkward moment. She now had to except the fact another woman could influence her children (this is not so easy when it is happening to you). Yet, she had to trust her ex's decision like she was asking him to do with her decision. These adjustments are very, very difficult and take lot of prayer, conversation, and understanding.

One year, my wife and I went to Houston, Texas and we took my bonus son with us. We stopped in Memphis, TN to see my two sons and my bonus son stayed with my ex wife. To say it more clearly, my wife left her biological son with my ex wife. This is how a blended family should operate. He had a great time playing with his bonus brothers (my biological children) and my ex-wife made sure he was well taken care of. This is the level of commitment you want to have with your blended family. If you choose your new partner wisely, you will be able to reach this.

When my son turned thirteen years old, he moved to Cleveland from Memphis and became a permanent part of our family. This was a huge adjustment for all of us. Before, my wife only had to deal with her children; now she had to deal with my son who brought a whole new dynamic to the family. I was a little more of a disciplinarian than my wife and my son perceived my wife was a lot more lenient towards her children than she was to him. For years, we had to deal with making sure we were fair with all of the children. No matter what we did, someone always was unhappy. When you have children from different parents living in the same house, I suggest you post a cleaning schedule on the wall. This shows the children you are being fair and not making your bonus children do all of the work. When your biological children are gone to see their other family for the weekend, do some fun things with your bonus children, show them they are special to you too. Show them a little more love and care to win them over. You must be fair in the love you share.

It was a welcome moment for me when my son came to live with us because I had someone I could relate to. I could let my guard down, be myself, and pour my love into my son without any reservations. Now, again, my wife had the same opportunity to understand the level of commitment it takes to love someone else's child as your own. This takes dedication on behalf of the adults in the children's lives. If you are reading this book and you have a bonus mom or dad who made a sacrifice to raise you and love you, they deserve a huge hug of gratitude.

All graduations are grand events in our house—elementary school, middle school, high school, and college. My wife is huge on education and she wanted to celebrate the children's accomplishments. When graduations happened, all the family came out on both side with bells on. My wife's family and her ex-husband's family attended in large numbers. My wife's ex-husband's mom (the kids' grandmother) and his sister (the kids' aunt) were especially visible. (I speak about them to let you know they have a right to be there to support the children as well.) Then my wife's family, her mother, aunt and uncle, brothers and sister, also attended. It was a family reunion and all of these people knew each other having had years to cultivate their relationships. In a situation like this, it would be easy for the new partner, i.e. me, to feel like the odd man out. Yet, all of these people should be there to support the children who have accomplished one of these milestones in their lives.

How do you handle this kind of situation? You smile a lot and be a support to your wife and your bonus child, without getting in the way of the extended family. You take a step back without trying to be the center of attention and don't demand your wife place you at the center of the action. Believe me, everyone knows you are there and you will earn respect in time. I recommend finding a way to participate and be involved. I became the photographer and the person who recorded the event on dvd. I wanted to contribute but not be overbearing. These are difficult moments and you have to put things in their proper place so you don't feel insignificant. I must admit, the first few events I felt out of place and sort of on the outside looking in. These people all knew each other; they were laughing and talking and I was just there. I would interact with my wife's family, however, and whenever they asked a question, I would answer very politely. I understood how important it was to win them over so my children would not feel any tension between us. When my son moved in with me, these events became a little easier because the children would include him in the conversations with their family and, ultimately, I was pulled into the conversation. At the events of your bonus children, your job is support your partner with lots of love and patience.

As you continue to love on your wife and her children, your new in-laws will warm up to you and when these events take place they will began to include you into the mix naturally. What I've said about my wife's events is reversed when it comes to my family functions. She has to do everything I have described and be a support for me as my ex-wife's family comes to my children's event. The more you participate in these events, the more you will get to know the family and, as the children speak highly of you, the family will receive you. At the end of the day, all the family wants is for the children to be happy. When the children go to the grandmother's home of the ex, they are being asked about you, the new partner. If those kids give a good report, or at least not a bad one, the family will warm up to you. Therefore, when you go to the next family event, they will began to be a little more inviting.

If the children do not like you, however, and let the family know you are not a loving person, the family will give you a cold shoulder and won't have anything to do with you. You do not want this to happen. Blending two families is challenging enough and you do not want enemies in the family if possible.

Whenever I attended an event, I allowed my wife and her ex-husband to interact with their child together and that child was glad to have both parents' attention. I was always there to support my wife, but the focus was on the child celebrating the event. I would place my ego in check and not demand to be front and center of my wife's attention in these moments. I am big on the fact that children do not ask for their parents to divorce and they should not be punished for their parents' choices. They should get both parents at their events without any drama. If you don't like something that went on at the event, wait until you get home to talk about it.

I don't want to give you the illusion we were able to do this without incident. There were many times I did not like the way things went and sometimes I did not give off the best vibe. However, my wife and I talked about it and tried to come to some resolution. Remember, this is your new family and it is up to the both of you to work through the maze.

I eventually won over my wife's ex-husband, his mother, and his sisters; now we all have mutual respect for each other. When I say "win them over" I mean we all get along with no drama. The goal is not to be best friends; the goal is to have mutual respect. When my bonus daughter graduated from high school, we lived in New Orleans at the time. All of my wife's family and her ex-husbands' family flew out for the graduation. We had the graduation dinner catered and my wife and I were hosting the party at our home. Remember, this graduation took place many years into our relationship after we all had had time to cultivate relationships as a blended family.

As we went to the graduation, all of us sat in the same section. We had one goal in mind and that was to celebrate the graduation of my bonus daughter. Again, I assumed the position of recording the event on dvd because it gave me a sense of purpose. I was involved and participating, yet I was giving my wife and her ex-husband the opportunity to celebrate their daughter. It was a great day and my bonus daughter was proud to have all of her family and her dad come so far to be a part of her special day. I took a step back to allow her dad to have his proud moment without interference or placing any demands on my bonus daughter to recognize me.

Here is what I did to further help make this day special for my bonus daughter and wife. When the graduation ceremony was over, I left to go home while everyone was taking pictures at the school. I wanted to make sure the food was warm when they returned home and the caterers had everything together. Everyone was at the graduation celebration, but I was thinking of being a blessing to my bonus daughter, hanging all the decorations and balloons and making sure everything was prepared for when they returned home. This gesture caught the attention of my wife's ex-in-laws and they welcome me into the family from that day forward. I had showed them I wanted this day to be special for them as well as my daughter. (By the way, I love them just as much, they are incredible people.) From that day forward, they have become my family as well and when they come to Orlando they are welcome to stay in our home. Blended families can work on all levels, however, you have to be committed to the challenge.

You have to be willing to go beyond the call of duty sometimes to make the situation work for the good of your family. I have always believed children deserve the best possible life we can give them. At their events, we must do everything we can to make it a special occasion for them. It does not cost you anything to be nice; even if someone is looking for drama, don't play into their hands. Stay focused on the event and put your best foot forward so nothing is said or done that you will regret. We were blessed that no one in the family was difficult in anyway. May I suggest that if you know someone in your family will cause a scene and ruin your child's day, politely ask them not to come. It is important you build a healthy family and a safe environment for your kids.

I want to share one more event that touched my heart very much. It was time for my bonus daughter to be married. She came to me and asked if I would participate in walking her down the aisle. I would walk her half way down the aisle and her biological dad would walk her the rest of the way. This was a huge deal for me and represents how my bonus daughter and I have come a long way. Remember, she is a daddy's girl even today. This was a tough relationship to form together and I made a lot of mistakes as a bonus dad. Over the years, there were many situations we had to overcome to get to this point. To be requested to walk her down the aisle on her wedding day was a huge accomplishment. Everything we worked so hard to achieve paid off. When your bonus daughter ask you to walk her down the aisle on her big day, you did something right. We hung in there together and beat all odds to love each other through some challenging moments.

As much as I thought it was sweet of her to ask me, I believe one of the dreams of a father is to walk his daughter down the aisle. I never had a daughter from my own seed, however she is the bonus daughter God has allowed in my life. However, her biological dad was alive and I felt this was his big moment. I did not want to steal any part of this special time he so rightly and fully deserved. He is a great father and he loves his daughter very much. By the way, this is his only daughter and I recognized he would never get this opportunity again. I shared with my daughter that I was so honored she asked me, but I believed her father should do the honors. I asked what could I do and still be a part of the wedding day.

At this time, I had become the pastor of a church I started in Orlando, FL, called the Christian Family Worship Center (www.cfwcorlando.com). She asked me to do the ceremony instead. This way her dad had the privilege of walking her down the aisle and her bonus dad had the opportunity to perform the wedding. This is the way blended families are supposed to work. What a great day for everyone! My bonus daughter had the best of both worlds. I said "who give our daughter to be married to this man," and her father said "we do!"

Likewise, my biological son was married, and my ex-wife came from Memphis, TN to be a part of the wedding. When it was time to light the unity candle, my wife took the supporting role and allowed his mother to take the lead. His mother walked down the aisle and sat in the groom's seat. As the co-pastor of our church, my wife participated in the wedding ceremony along with me. At the reception, when it was time for the mother and son dance, my son took his biological mother's hand and danced with her, as my wife sat at the table watching. In the middle of the song, my son politely escorted his mother to her seat and came over to his bonus mom and finished out the song, dancing with her. We all were up laughing and having a good time together celebrating our son's day. All of my ex-wife's family was there and we all had a great time being a blended family. This is the goal of the blended family—no drama, just love and support for the well-being of each other.

Here is an important part you should be prepared for. There needs to be two sets of pictures at these events; one set with the biological parents and family, and one set with your bonus family. Sometimes, due to the stress of the day, you want to get picture taking over and done with. However, make sure you take time out to include the entire family in their own set of pictures. Make sure that when introducing the parents, you introduce all of them. In other words, prepare for everyone, not leaving anyone out. I am speaking about the immediate and bonus family.

I have given you a few examples on how we handled situations that came up in our family. Do what works for your family but make sure the people you are celebrating are not dealing with negativity from outside forces. Be on your best behavior and keep your egos in check; it not about you, it about your new family. Discuss any problems that may arise when you get to the privacy of your own home so the next event will be a better experience. My wife and I still discuss what we may have felt uncomfortable dealing with.

If you make sure to put the children first, you will receive huge rewards. My daughter has giving us two grandbabies and do you know who they are crazy about? Yep, their papa, ME! Yes, they love all of their family, but I hold a special place in their hearts. Now my sons have children and they are a great part of our lives as well. They don't know anything about bonus papa as I have been their papa from day one. They refuse to hear step anything; we are one family and that's all that matters to them. They love their biological grandfather and they love me; in their eyes there is no different between the two of us. We have moved onto the next generation and what was a blended family has become simply a family. If you put the work into it, you will receive the rewards from it. Let me encourage you; you can do it. Hang in there and your life will be blessed from the effort. Your children will rise up and call you blessed.

CHAPTER 9

Family Crisis

"Faith makes all things possible.
Hope makes all things work. Love makes all things beautiful."
Author Unknown

Let's look at how a blended family should deal with very sensitive issues, such as illness, tragedies, hospital visits, or the death of a love one. There are so many "normal" things that cause tension in a blended family, it's important to consider how to handle the extraordinary situations as well. I want to give you a few suggestions on how to handle these moments.

To be in a blended family, you have to be secure about your relationship with your new spouse. Trust is imperative to creating a healthy family and if that trust is broken it will be very difficult to hold your family together. A traditional marriage has a hard time over coming betrayal. In a blended family, it is that much harder. I am reminded of my wife having to go to London with her ex-husband to be with my bonus son. If I did not trust my wife in this situation, we would have had major problems concerning this matter.

It was a serious situation. My bonus son had moved to London, England to complete his Master's degree. While in London, he became ill and had to go into the hospital. We had no family over there and the doctors were not sure what was wrong with him. My wife wanted to rush to his bedside to be with him. Truth be told, my bonus son was very nervous and wanted his mother there as well. His dad wanted to be there too. When we looked at the cost of airline tickets to fly from Orlando to London on such short notice, it was very, very expensive. We had to make a decision; would we both go together or was she going to go alone with her ex-husband to see their son. Since we could not afford for both of us to go, my wife went alone.

When I tell this story during my seminars, there are always a few men in the crowd who say, "Not my wife, she would not be going anywhere with her ex." I had to place my bonus son's well-being above everything else. It would have been wrong of me to add to my wife's stress and agony with my insecurity during this challenging time. My bonus son was in trouble and my wife needed to get to London to see him. What if something tragic was to happen? My wife would never forgive me and I would never forgive myself. His well-being was of foremost importance. The reason my wife was able to see to her son without problems from me was because I trusted she was not interested in getting back together with her ex. If I did not trust her or if she had a past of infidelity, this would have been a bigger problem in our marriage.

It is important for you to make sure your new partner feels secure in your relationship so that if a crisis moment happens, your partner will be able to support you without a lot of drama. During the good times, make sure you love on each other so trust can be built for the times of crisis. Your relationship must be able to weather such moments when they happen. If you can't trust your partner to be faithful, you have greater problems; a crisis is only going to seriously expose those issues.

When they arrived in London, my wife and her ex-husband stayed with their son's friend in separate bedrooms. They were able to see about their son and assure him everything would be all right. We discovered he was having some internal bleeding and the doctors in London were not sure why. We felt it best to return him back to the States to have him under the care of the doctor we felt more comfortable with attending to his health. My bonus son returned home and was taken to the hospital in Cleveland, Ohio. The doctor was able to properly diagnose his condition and it was determined surgery was needed.

I was able to join the entire family at the hospital on the day of surgery. My bonus son's entire family came to the hospital to support him—his dad, his dad's wife, his dad's mother and sisters, my wife and our family, her brothers, sisters, and cousins. All of the family was there to support him in this serious situation. There was no room for any of us to be cynical or sarcastic, our partners needed our support, not any disgruntled attitudes. This is the dynamics of the blended family; when you understand your roles, you are able to carry them out in love.

After the surgery was complete, the doctor came out and said only the parents could come back into the patient's room. My wife and my bonus son's father jumped up. I was not offended because I understood my role was to support my wife. I was not acting in place of the father to my bonus son because his dad was there to fulfill that role. Before I knew it, something amazing happened. After about an hour of them visiting their son, his father came out to me and invited me to go in to see him because I have been such a huge support to his son and I have loved him as my own. When I understood my role, there was no fight to be had during this sensitive time. I went in to see my bonus son and spend time with him in prayer.

When he was moved to a room, all four of us—my wife and I, his dad and his wife—all worked together to get our son back to health. There were times all of us would be in the room loving on our son, laughing together, creating a healthy environment for our son to get well. The last thing our son needed was for us to be at each other throats arguing and bickering about our insecurities. We focused on the well-being of our son and not the drama of the family dynamics. When you experience these kinds of situations, you have to work to make them an amicable experience.

For my bonus daughter, the hospital experience was very different because she was giving birth to our first grandson in New Orleans, while her dad was living in Cleveland. Now I became the primary father taking the leading role alongside my wife. We were united together at the hospital to support our daughter. I looked to see what I could do to support the family so we all could have a happy, memorable experience.

Since my bonus daughter was also living with us in New Orleans, I worked with her mother to get the baby's room ready. This is my bonus grandson, but since I was there at his birth, it feels as if he is my biological grandbaby. I dropped the bonus grandson title and received him into my heart as my very own grandson. Why is there a change now? It's because I invested into his mother, my bonus daughter, as if she were my own child and now receive this grandbaby as the fruit of that hard work. My wife was so excited for this new addition to the family I became excited as well. I made sure I added things to the baby's room so I would have an invested interested in the child.

Some might question why go through all this in a blended family if it is so much work or a lot of drama. Let me counter, if this was your biological child would anything stop you from being by your child side? In a blended family, no matter the road ahead, no matter how difficult the situation, you must put forth an effort to resolve any conflicts that may arise. The reason you put in all of the work is because you never give up on your biological family and children. I never gave up on my bonus children because they truly are my children. When I married their mother, I made a commitment to her children as well. You have to find a way to make your blended family work at all costs. Especially during times of crisis, families need each other. You cannot check out of the process and think you are going to have a happy marriage with your wife alone. If you don't support the children in times of crisis, you will lose your partner. Mothers and real men can't separate themselves from their children. If you dislike a person's child, you have ultimately rejected the person.

On the day our grandbaby was born, my wife and I were at the hospital waiting with anticipation. With his birth, our lives changed forever and all the hard work paid off. I remember holding him in the hospital and he opened up his eyes and smiled at me. I said to my wife, "This baby is laughing and smiling at me." My wife told me it was not possible because babies don't laugh or smile when they are first born. I said, "Well you better look at this baby, he is smiling at his Papa." From that day forward, he and I have been inseparable; he has been a huge gift from God to our family. This baby healed the hearts of everyone in the family. I began to experience something I didn't think was possible—that I could love someone just as much as I loved my biological children. I forgot all about bonus grandson and he became my grandson for real. I believe when my bonus daughter saw how much I loved her child, I was able to purchase a real place in her heart and our relationship changed forever, which further gives credence to my claim, when you love someone's child, they will love you more.

When your bonus children really see you love them for real in the good times and bad, you will be able to find a permanent home in their hearts. I spoil my grandson so much he is rotten. He brought us together as one family; we all have one goal in mind and that is his well-being. Christmas has not been the same since he came into our lives. When the family has one goal they can work towards, it will bring everyone together. For us, it was this grandbaby.

He is now a teenager as I write this book. He knows all of his other grandparents and he loves them all. I told him I was his step grandfather and he refused to receive it. He knows it's true, however, he says I am never allowed to say that to him. You see what love can do when you press through all of the stuff and drama? Blended families can work and you will be blessed by all of your children if you invest love in them as your own children.

If my daughter's biological dad had been in town doing the birth of her son, I would have taken a back seat to him so he could welcome his first grandbaby into the world. I am trying to show you through these stories how we have conducted ourselves in our blended family and have had some success. I knew a family who did not display this kind of love; the family was unhealthy and produced unhealthy children as well. The husband choose to be married to the woman and not deal with her children and the mother allowed him to conduct himself in this matter.

This man refused to celebrate anything that had to do with his wife's children. The only birthday he acknowledged was his own; he never purchased a gift or a card or showed the children any love. He was so overwhelmingly concerned and jealous of the biological father that he equated showing love to the children as showing support for their dad. This man did not allow their mother to be there for her children, and when the children became adults they turned on him and did not support her. The son told me they would not take any more of his "bullship". That's what he said—all the bull he placed on their ship, they refused to carry any longer. Again, you as the new partner should not demand a woman choose you over her children. Any woman that does that is a fool in my opinion. Your children are the greatest gift God can ever give you. You must guard their hearts with everything within you. If a man does not want to be with your children, then he does not want to be with you.

In family crisis, you may have a child sick with an illness that requires the family's full attention. Your partner may have dinner reservations at an expensive restaurant, but if your child has an asthma attack and is rushed to the hospital, you should go and attend to the child's needs. You should pay attention to this while you are dating to see if your partner comes with you to support you or sends you on your own. If they send you on your own, you may need to find someone who is more sensitive to the needs of your ill child. Taking care of an ill child takes a lot of prayer and patience; you need someone who is willing to support you. If by chance you do have somebody that loves and supports you, please love them because they are hard to come by. You need someone who will stand with you and your children, however, they should know how to step up when needed and how to step back if the biological parent comes to the hospital as well.

My son is dealing with this in his marriage. He has two bonus children with health issues and he has been a champion in putting their needs first. There have been times both of his bonus children have been hospitalized. He has had to follow the steps I've laid out in this book; to be there to support their mother, but step back when the biological father comes to see about his child. Because the children have health issues, it is very important the bonus dad and biological dad communicate. For example, when the children come home from their biological father's, my son needs to know when was the last time they received their meds and how is their blood pressure. He needs to know if there are any concerns. If you don't have a good working relationship in a situation like this, it could mean the death of a child. You have to put all jealousy and insecurity aside to do what is best for the children. My son comes from a blended family; he saw my example and I am proud to say he is doing a great job. He has learned it is hard work to navigate through all of the personalities but he is succeeding at the task.

Funerals are another family crisis but you can handle them in pretty much the same way. To God be the glory that we have not had to deal with this in my immediate household, however, I have dealt with these issues as a pastor. In one situation, a man had a daughter he just adored (remember daughters are daddy's girls). The bonus mom seemed to be jealous of the relationship and did not try to connect with the daughter. When the father would go out of town for business, the wife stayed on one side of the house and the daughter stayed on the other. When the father spoke to his wife about the problem, she would say she wasn't going to deal with a child that had an attitude all of the time. "She is a child and I am the adult; she needs to respect my house."

This woman did not follow my advice to never go down to the level of the child. In fact, she starting saying things like "Maybe your daughter should move in with her biological mother. Seems she can't respect my house and, as I am the woman of the house, she needs to leave." This is not the way to handle these feelings; you should never, ever tell your partner their children are not welcome into your home.

As life would have it, one evening the daughter was in an accident and killed by a drunk driver. The dad was devastated by the news and was inconsolable. The last person he wanted to be around him was his wife. All the hate and venom that had come from her mouth could not be taken back. The wife tried to explain she did not mean what she had said, however, it was too late. All the father could remember was what the bonus mother said about his daughter and this time it was unforgivable. The father grieved without the support of his wife and I don't need to tell you the outcome of this marriage; they eventually divorced. Whenever you reject someone's child, they will ultimately reject you. Find a way to connect to the children and win them over. It won't always be easy but it is possible.

When my wife lost her mother, her ex-husband attended the service because he was a part of the family. He was there to support his children who lost their grandmother. I was busy consoling my wife; I welcomed him to be there to console our children. The children needed their biological father during this time of crisis because they were still very young at the time. The last thing my wife needed was for me to be making a scene over her ex-husband being at the service.

Years later my wife's aunt was admitted to the hospital and the doctors gave her less than forty-eight hours to live. Remember, my wife's ex-husband had been a part of her life for the last thirty-five years. When my wife and ex-husband divorced, my wife's ex-husband lived in an apartment above my wife's aunt for many years. Just because my wife decided to end the relationship, her family was under no obligation to follow suit. When the ex-husband purchased his home, he was only a mile away from where this aunt lived. He would go over to her house to check on her because he had established a relationship long before I came into the picture. When my wife and I moved to New Orleans, he was still the one going by to check on my wife's aunt.

When we received the call concerning my wife's aunt, we arrived at the hospital to sit by her side in the final hours of her life. I now had been a part of my wife's aunt's life for more than twenty-five years myself. We prayed and cried together, waiting for her to make her transition. My wife's ex-husband also came to the hospital, however, this time he stepped back and I took the lead because this was about my wife. He was there because of his relationship with the aunt and to comfort his children. To deny him the opportunity to come and say goodbye to someone he had a relationship with for over thirty-five years would have been petty on my part. After twenty-five years of blending the family together, we pretty much have this routine down. After she passed away, during the funeral, I sat next to my wife and he sat next to his kids in that section of the family. Why? Because we are a blended family and this is what family does. Whenever you go to a funeral, all of the family should be able to come together to support one another.

This also happened when my ex-wife's mother passed. My wife and I went to Memphis, TN to support my ex-wife's family and support my sons. We sat in the family section because I had known my ex-wife's mother for over thirty-five years. Even though my ex-wife and I had been divorced for over thirty years, my ex-wife's mother still called me her son. All of my ex-wife's nieces and nephews still call me Uncle Jerry today. Why was my wife and I at my ex-wife's mother funeral? Because we are a blended family! At the service, the family asked me to say some words and give expressions of love. I was happy to do so and it would have been heartbreaking of them if they thought not to make room for me to speak.

Some may ask how far you should go in blending a family together. I do think it's asking a little too much to have your ex's name in your family obituary, but if you want them to share words, I think that is appropriate. To have them come over to the repasts would be in order as well. You can work together to bring the family comfort during these difficult times. You want to make it as easy as possible so drama won't become the issue with all of the pain the family is already experiencing.

I suggest during any family crisis you seek help from a professional marriage counselor or pastor. Some of the decisions you make in these moments can have a profound effect on the way you live. When you are in a lot of pain, you may not be able to make rational decisions and therefore seeking outside help can guide your family along. Blended families have a difficult time under normal circumstances; with a major crisis it can be unbearable. With the help of God and prayer, I know you will be able to get tough times and grow closer together. It will take work and patience, but as I have said, you can get through it.

CHAPTER **10**

Living with Regrets
Serves No Purpose

Don't carry your mistakes around with you.
Instead, place them under your feet and
use them as stepping stones.
Never regret. If it's good, it's wonderful. If it's bad, it's experience.
Author Unknown

"Forgiving yourself is a requirement to becoming a healthy family"

There is harm in living with past regrets of guilt and un-forgiveness. My wife and I have both talked about how we wish we would have done things a little different for our children. We saw the effects of our divorces manifest as the children came into adulthood. When your children become adults, there is a new set of challenges that come with the territory. For some reason, I thought after we got the kids graduated from high school, they would be off to college and we would live happy ever after. Oh, how

I was wrong. The effects of the divorces that had been suppressed when the children were younger began to emerge in their adult behavior.

We must understand the decisions we make will in some ways affect our children in the future. I know children can go astray in tradition families, however in a blended family, when your children veer off the right track, you have a tendency to question why and began to blame yourself. Do any of these statements seem familiar?

1. Maybe if I did not get a divorce from their father/mother.
2. Maybe if I hadn't worked long hours.
3. I should have brought them up in the church.
4. I should have never left them with that person.
5. I should have never remarried until they were grown.

We can go on and on with the list of things we should have done that might have influenced our children to make better decisions. These are just a few things we say as we blame ourselves for some of the behaviors our children display.

In order to remove this guilt and discouragement, we need to receive the unconditional love offered to us through forgiveness. No parent does the job of raising their children perfectly. There is only one perfect Father and He lives in heaven. He loves you and wants to help you through the guilt and shame that have come from your mistakes. If your heavenly Father can forgive you of your mistakes, surely you can forgive yourself of the choices you have made so your family can have the best possible chance to become healthy and whole.

When I look over my life, I can see where I made some decision stemming from the effects of my mother's and father's divorce. When you come from a divorced family, those dynamics will carry over into your adult life. You may find yourself having trust issues due to what you experienced as a child. The lack of trust could leave you feeling vulnerable and insecure as you go through life.

Carl Pickhardt, Ph.D. is a psychologist in Austin, Texas. Read what he shared in a blog post on Dec 19, 2011 in Surviving (Your Child's) Adolescence

> What I can do is try to distinguish some general ways children (up through about age 8 or 9) often react to parental divorce in contrast to how adolescents (beginning around ages 9–13) often respond. Understand that I am talking here about tendencies, not certainties.

Divorce introduces a massive change into the life of a boy or girl no matter what the age. Witnessing loss of love between parents, having parents break their marriage commitment, adjusting to going back and forth between two different households, and the daily absence of one parent while living with the other, all create a challenging new family circumstance in which to live. In the personal history of the boy or girl, parental divorce is a watershed event. Life that follows is significantly changed from how life was before.

Somewhat different responses to this painful turn of events occur if the boy or girl is still in childhood or has entered adolescence. Basically, divorce tends to intensify the child's dependence and it tends to accelerate the adolescent's independence; it often elicits a more regressive response in the child and a more aggressive response in the adolescent."

This article shows that even experts say divorce will affect your children in some way. As a young man, I deceived myself by saying I was not affected by my parents getting divorced. Upon self-examination, I realized I was a mess and needed to work through what was a lie and what was the truth.

Some of the effects may be that you find yourself attracted to older men/women trying to fill role that was vacant from the divorce of your parents. You may become a people pleaser, trying to always get people to like you as a result of the rejection you may have internalized from the divorce. Rejection can be a huge issue in your life which may be the effect of divorce showing up in your adult life and relationships.

If the father was absent in the home, a woman may have a challenge in relating to and trusting men. When it comes to understanding the behavior of a young man, she may not be able to relate because there was no male role model. This may have some negative effects on how she communicates with her partner and in raising her sons.

A man raised without a father may not know how to be a man, husband, or father to his own children. This will in some way show up in his relationship with his wife. He may deceive himself to believe he was not affected at all and that he turned out alright without his father in his life. If he is absent from his children's life due to the fact he did not have a father in his life, he may deem this behavior justified. He may begin to model the behavior shown to him when growing up. He may say, "Well, I turned out ok without my father, so if I'm not around my children, they will be ok." Let me assure you, anyone who has had an absent mother or father has been affected in a huge way. Now, I am not saying single parents don't do a great job is raising their children. There are many mothers who have raised sons to become great men in this world. I believe, however, no one can take the place of a father or mother in a child's life.

Divorce has a profound effect on our behavior and most of us are in denial about it. I was so wrong to believe that; I was in denial. I married at the age of eighteen years old. I lacked a loving home and went to seek it out in the first girl who said she loved me. You make irrational decisions when you find someone who says they love you when you are not getting love from home. As a child, I was very sensitive and got my feeling hurt easily. Where do you think this stems from? I had a lack of confidence and was afraid of rejection. When I did the work on my personal life, I realized all of these things came from my childhood. I was profoundly affected by the divorce. When my parents divorced, I interpreted the failure of their marriage as a rejection of me. To this day, I have to remind myself when I am denied, it does not mean I have been personally rejected.

Now that I am aware, I look at our children and wonder what did my wife and I do to effect the lives of our children.

Sometime divorce is unavoidable and is no fault of your own. Whether it is unavoidable or intentional, however, it still affects the children involved. All four of our children made mistake and seemed to not make the best choices for their lives early on. We kept asking ourselves how much of their decisions were just about being young and how much was the hidden effects of the divorces. All of their decisions could have been because of their youth and the times in which we lived. In our minds, we believed we somehow contributed to the wrong path they were taking. We began to feel guilty for what was taking place in their lives. At times, we would make excuses for some of the things they were doing in order to justify our decisions to help them out of their mistakes. Any good parent knows that after your children reach the age of eighteen years old you have to make an adjustment and get ready to release them into the real world with your guidance.

Without getting into details about each one of our children, let me just say all of them went "Ziggy-d-Boo." That is my wife's famous saying. She does not say that the kids have gone crazy; she says that they have gone "Ziggy-d-Boo." Each one of them wanted to do the opposite of what was modeled in front of them.

My wife and I always wanted to model a great family in front of our children, but how the children internalized it was open for their own interpretation. I found this out when our children became older and they would tell us how they saw a decision we made they disagreed with. Their recollection was totally different from what actually happened or the way my wife and I saw it. These moments are unavoidable because each and every one of us are entitled to our own opinions. However, when someone's opinion become their reality, it becomes their truth and ultimately shapes their behavior. They live out their truth according to how they see the truth for them.

If your children blame you for the divorce, you have to help them see your truth and walk through this period of time until they forgive you in this area. Maturity sometimes does not happen until they get married and have children of their own. Then they may be able to see how difficult life can be raising children.

These were difficult years we had to navigate through. Remember what I said about having rented space in your bonus children hearts? Well, when they turn eighteen years old, they determine whether or not to evict you or downsize your space all together. All four of our children wanted to make it known they were grown and could make their own decisions without any advice from us. Now, again, this could be what happens in a traditional family, however in a blended family there are a lot of unspoken, buried, suppressed feelings waiting to be released and expressed. Often, what is said is magnified greater than it probably is. When your biological children say "I hate you" in a traditional family, you let it blow over and say "Oh well, they will get over it." You don't take it to heart because you know kids say things when they are upset they do not mean. However, when your bonus children say the same thing, you go through a lot of emotions and their comments are magnified. I want to tell you as the children get older, they will have the boldness to tell you how they really feel. Don't magnify it too much try and allow what is said to roll off your back. I think all children when they reach the ages of sixteen to twenty-five lose their minds and think they know it all. To them, all parents are stupid and don't know anything. I would suggest you let what they say roll off your back and keep on being a loving parent. If you need to apologize for something you may have done please do so.

My wife and I felt we made tremendous sacrifices to give our children the best life possible. There were days we went without so our children could have what they needed. There were moments we fought in silence. We went through unnecessary drama with ex's to fight on their behalf. I can go on and on about the things we've done to give our children a better life. Yet, at the end of all of the sacrifices made, like most children, they could not comprehend what was done on their behalf. None of the sacrifices we made counted for them at this time of their lives. They wanted to be free from all of the rules and restrictions of the family so they could do whatever it was they wanted to do.

Our children seemed to rebel against our authority and blame us for all of the wrong that happened in their lives. This sent both of us to question whether or not we made the right decision in forcing them to come together as a blended family. We started questioning should we have stay with our ex's for the children's sake. I remember us saying if we could go back again we would not have gotten divorced. We were convinced the pain of watching our children go down the wrong road was more painful than sticking it out with our ex's. All of these feeling are a result of guilt you must overcome and deal with.

I remember very early in my divorce, my ex-wife moved back to Memphis, TN while I stayed in Cleveland, Ohio. I came to visit my sons and the younger one was not doing well at school. He was in the 2nd or 3rd grade. He had spent the first half of the school year living in Cleveland near me and his report card had been A's and B's. I went to visit the teacher concerning the change in his behavior and grades. The teacher showed me his grades and when I looked at his report card he had straight Fs. I was horrified and heartbroken that he had completely shut down.

What in the world happened? Then it hit me like a ton of bricks. The thing that had changed was his parents' marriage. The divorce rocked his little world. When your children have to deal with this type of loss, it will profoundly affect them and you need to be prepared to support them at all costs. From that day forward, my son struggled to make the adjustment and it carried over into his adulthood. I was not aware enough to get him the help he needed to deal with this loss as a child; I was only in my mid-twenties myself.

Many years later, I was looking at pictures with my boys. In the pictures, my younger son was around five years old and my older son was around seven years old. Now they were young men in their twenties during this moment of reflection. I wished I could have gone back and done it all over again. I felt guilty I left my children uncovered when they moved to Memphis. I was their father and it was my responsibility to raise them into great men. When you feel like this, remorse sets in and you begin to make decisions that may not be the best for your children. You start working and doing things for them out of guilt. You have to take a breath, get your head together, and make sound decisions outside these feelings to help your children and not handicap their growth.

I believe my wife and I took two different directions in this matter of dealing with our guilt. After many years, we came back together in how we handle these issues in a more practical and healthy way. Please understand it is an ongoing process, even today. For a long time, we did not take a balanced approach to the way we handled issues with our children.

None of us want to see our children struggle through challenging times, however, the experience of struggle is necessary to help them to fly through life. Let me share this story:

There was a little boy who saw a butterfly struggling to break out of its cocoon. It was struggling and struggling but it was having a huge challenge getting out of the shell. The little boy went into the kitchen, pulled out a knife, and ran back outside to cut open the cocoon to set the butterfly free. The little boy opened up the cocoon so that the butterfly trapped inside could fly away but to his surprise, the butterfly did not fly but died on the ground instead.

The little boy was horrified the butterfly died and it may have been killed by his hands. He ran into the house crying to his grandfather, "Please help me." The grandfather ran outside to see what had upset the boy so much, only to find the dead butterfly. The little boy explained to his grandfather what happened. The little boy said, "I saw this butterfly struggling to get out of his cocoon and I wanted to help him so I cut open the cocoon to set him free so he could fly away. When I cut him out, the butterfly died instead of flying."

The grandfather answered, "Do you know why it died?" The little boy said no so the grandfather continued. "Oh son, that butterfly needed to struggle. When the butterfly struggles to get out of the cocoon it strengthens its wings to fly. When you cut him out, you did not allow him to struggle and get the strength to fly, so he died. The struggle is necessary to get the strength to fly."

When our children become adults, we continue to cut them out of their troubles and situations very early on in their adulthood. When my wife and I look back over those decisions, we question how many of them we made out of guilt. I can say there were times we should have let our children think their way out of challenging moments and situations.

Yet, because we did not balance it with tough love, we were not helping our children to gain the strength to fly.

On the other hand, I know people who cut their children off the day they turn eighteen years old. I knew of a family whose step-dad wanted the kids out of the house and did not want to care for them. As soon as the son turned eighteen, the father put him out to make it on his own. In my opinion, this is cruel and it's unreasonable to think any kid can make it on their own at this age. The father said to me "My mother did it to me and I made it; it will teach him to be a man." I asked how his relationship with his mother was currently. He admitted they were not close. You see, you can treat your children this way but to think you will have a great relationship with them after you put them out in the cold is a gross miscalculation. There is an adjustment period a child must be helped through as they become an adult. If there's ever a time your children need your guidance, it is during the ages of sixteen to twenty-five. The world is cruel and cold, waiting to devour your children's lives. That man's son ended up robbing and shooting a store clerk. His son is spending the rest of his life in jail. In my opinion, this is not the way to grow your children up into adulthood, putting them out the house the day they turn eighteen years old.

That is the extreme, but I believe you must find a balance. You have to make children earn their way and not give them everything they ask for. You must require they get a job and teach them how to budget and manage a check book. You must teach them about credit scores and paying bills on time. You must teach them the important of saving money and purchasing a home.

These are only a few things you need to cover. I would recommend you demand they take a Dave Ramsey money management course. If I had this information at an early age, my life would have been much different. These are the ways you lead your children from childhood to adulthood, not put them out of the house and tell them to do the best they can on their own.

No one is a perfect parent. We all have made mistakes and done things we wish we could take back. You have to forgive yourself, refuse to live with the guilt, and do better now that you know better. Don't handicap your children by not allowing them to figure out some of life's curve balls on their own. If for some reason you owe them an apology, give it to them and do everything you can to love them. Guilt serves no purpose but to imprison you from living your best life now. If there is someone you need to forgive, do so or you will be drinking the poison of death. TD Jakes said, "unforgiveness is like drinking poison hoping the other person will die." The one who eventually will die is you.

Do the best you can to love and raise your children and don't let guilt guide your decisions. It is not a healthy way to raise your children and help them stand on their own to deal with life. You have to balance helping them without enabling them. If you don't keep this balance, you will allow your children to use guilt to manipulate you and it will hurt everyone in the end.

I want to share one more point concerning adult children. At this moment in your life, your focus needs to change from your children to your partner. Your partner should be first in your life and your children should be a part but not controlling your life. Let me caution the new partner: this in no way means your spouse should have to forsake their children to have a relationship with you. All the children should be welcome in your home and made to feel like family at all times. They should not continue to be, however, the focus of your attention at this time of your life.

I have seen too many instances where marriages have dissolved because the biological parent could not stop taking care of their grown children out of guilt. Usually mothers have a hard time cutting the strings. You have to allow your children to grow without paying their way through life. It's okay to help your children out, all of us need a hand up sometimes, however you must find a balance or this will cause problems in your family.

I want to be very clear; I am not talking about a partner who wants you to forsake your flesh and blood. I have experienced some people who don't want you to have anything to do with your adult children at all. They get upset when you purchase anything and give it to your child. They want you to cut off your children on their 18th birthday as if you can just stop loving them. This person is being unreasonable and unrealistic.

On the other hand, if you are still helping your thirty-five year old child by paying their rent and car note every month, this is a problem. To expect your partner not to say anything is also unreasonable and unrealistic. There has to be a balance in order to have a healthy relationship with your grown children. Otherwise you will cause your children not to like your partner and you will blame your partner for cutting them off. Please do not use this tactic as an excuse to take the responsibility of being a parent your partner cannot be seen as the reason you have stopped paying for your grown children's lifestyles. If you make your partner the fall person, your grown children will despise him or her for cutting them off, and you will never have the happy blended family you are trying to create. You must make sure your own children know it is your decision alone to stop funding them.

One family I helped had a son who would get a job and then quit because he did not like his hours. When he quit, his mother would pay his rent until he found another job. He would work a few months and quit again. He would go to school for a few semesters and then drop out of school. His mother would send him money again and again, telling her husband if she didn't help him out then who would. It continued. When he was arrested for an altercation, his mother bailed him out of jail. When he needed a lawyer for his court appearance, she paid the entire bill. She did all of this as a result of years of guilt because she divorced his father when he was a kid. This is an example of the manipulation and enabling I am speaking about.

I believe it is reasonable when your children graduate from high school to help them while they are in college for four years. That is a reasonable expectation. If you require your child to get a job and work their way through college, that is also reasonable. It may be hard on the child but that is the struggle that will give him or her the strength to fly. You owe your adult children much love and support, however, you do not owe them cars, credit cards, or houses. Guilt is an expensive thing to finance and support, not to mention the emotional toil it takes.

If you owe your children an apology for something you did wrong, you should give it to them freely. I believe in apologizing to my children if I am wrong. In fact, I believe in apologizing if they were offended by some of my decisions. I may have done what I did because it was the best option at that time, but it may have affected their lives in a negative way so I owe my children a sincere apology for my action. By apologizing, this should release the guilt you are feeling and you can begin to heal. If you don't give them the apology they deserve, it can cause friction in building a healthy relationship. My dad once said to me that children have feelings as they are just little people. When you realize they are people too you have to fix the wrong you may have caused them. This is important because once you ask them for forgiveness, you can release the guilt that has held you bound. Hopefully you can move past it and deal with your adult children from a healthy place.

You can't go back and change the past; the only thing you can do is grow towards the future. When your children began to date and start their relationships, they will see things a little differently. Life will teach them the decisions you made were not easy ones and they will began to appreciate you as their parent. They will began to understand the difficult role you played in their life as a bonus parent and you should see a little more appreciation for all you have done. If you continue to show love towards your adult children, I believe at some point they will return back and say thank you.

CHAPTER 11

Extended Family–Outside Children

"The more you take responsibility for your past and present,
the more you are able to create the future you seek."
Author Unknown

I n a blended family, how should you deal with children from other relationships? Hang with me as we go through some examples. Your ex may remarry and have children with their new partner. Your children now have brothers and sisters from another mother or father; this can become very complicated. Understand these children and your children are siblings.

Another scenario your spouse has been unfaithful to you during your marriage, and a child was born from this affair; it can be very challenging to accept the child who is a sibling to your children. In both instances, I want you to set aside your feelings and deal with the realities at hand. What is the proper way to look at these children as well as your children interaction with them?

Children are innocent and should not be punished for the acts of adults. I once knew a woman who had two sons and a daughter with her husband. The husband worked as a car salesman and one day sold a car to a women he later had an affair with. The woman became pregnant with his child and he had to tell his wife about the baby . You can imagine the anger and devastation this had on the wife and her family. She was angry with the husband and for months contemplated leaving him. She had three small children, however, and did not want to raise them without their father. The husband was regretful for his action and asked to be forgiven; he wanted to keep his family together.

With a baby soon to come the wife wanted nothing to do with her husband and did everything she could to put the baby out of her mind. The pain and memory was too much to bear. It is possible to walk away when it is just an affair, however, when a baby is involved, it is impossible; it is a whole new ballgame. The baby must be addressed. This is an incredibly difficult situation producing much pain that will be with the family for many years. What made this situation more challenging the husband was a man who believed in taking ownership of his mistakes. He wanted to be in his child's life because he believed it was the right thing to do. The wife was still in pain because of the betrayal and was within her full rights not to want to be a part of this fiasco. In addition, the husband's family was very fond of his wife and they also were very disappointed and angry. For the next few months, he and his wife sought help to repair the marriage and to look at the reason for the infidelity.

The couple created solutions and put some boundaries in place in hopes of avoiding this ever happening again. After the little girl was born, the husband sent financial support to the mother, when the child became a little older, about six months, he began going by the house and developing a relationship with her.

It is crucial and important for the husband to assure the wife he is only interested in his baby daughter and nothing else. Let me caution you, if you are not honest in your dealings, you will lose any hope of blending the child of your affair into your family. If you are going to see the child, you have to let your spouse know when and where this is going to take place. Even if she is upset, keep her informed of your decisions. If your spouse finds out you are sneaking over there even though it is honest, it could be perceived as cheating with the other person. Your spouse may be upset with you but it is the right thing to do in being responsible for caring for your child.

In time, the husband began to bring the new daughter over to his mother's house in order for her to meet his family. He continued to assure his wife he was only interested in taking care of the child, which again is the right thing to do. The wife was aware he was spending time with the child over at his mother's house. More importantly, his mother reassured the wife that the family is in full support of her. From this, the wife felt validated and understood which enabled her to very slowly soften her heart toward the child. This was a long, process and the husband was gentle and sensitive to the situation. Nothing happens overnight. By now, the wife had seen the girl several times and eventually agreed to allow the child to come over and spend the night. This was the beginning of an incredible relationship with the child being accepted by the entire family.

This was made possible because the husband reassured the wife of his commitment to their family. He was honest, remorseful, and continued to show his wife love. This took a lot of forgiveness, love, and plain hard work on his wife's part to open her heart to the child. The wife and husband were blending a new member into their family.

In time, the wife did something I had never seen. She welcomed this child into her home born out of her husband's affair and treated the child as if she was her very own. When I met the family, the man's daughter was twenty-two years old and I did not know the wife was the bonus mom until many years later. I was told by the girl's brothers and sister that they had never known of a time when she wasn't a part of the family. She would spend Christmas and Thanksgiving with them, she went on vacations — she was one of the family.

His wife, at some point, looked at the child and refused to punish her for the husband's behavior. The couple went on to have two more children and they all became one happy blended family. The child took it one step further and called the wife mom. The child, now an adult with her own family, with four children and all of them call the bonus mom grandmother and honor her with much love.

Sadly, the father passed away but the amazing part the daughter is still around giving and receiving love from his wife. His wife is an extraordinary human being; she turned her pain into love and it paid off in a great way. His wife understood that to take her anger out on an innocent child was not a loving thing to do. I would encourage you, if you have children that are outside of your marriage, to take a page from this woman's book. It could be a blessing to you in the future. Don't allow your anger or pain to deprive your children from knowing there other sibling. The child of the affair may be the very child that honors you in your later years. There a verse in the bible that says be not deceived whatsoever a person sows that is what they are going to reap. You get back what you put out, so I suggest you put out a lot of love. Your care taker may not be one of your own children but may be a child you loved as your own.

I want to share another example. A woman had two children from a previous marriage. She married a man who wanted nothing to do with her children. In time, they had three children of their own and the husband did nothing to promote his three children to have any relationship with the wife's other two children. The children grew up disliking one another and to this day they do not get along very well. The three children followed the example of their father; because he showed a dislike for his wife's other children, so did his children.

As life would have it the man in this story ended up having a heart attack. In the end, no one came to see him or care for him because he had not expressed love toward them. So, not only did the children dislike each other, they ultimately did not care for him. Let me share this saying with you, "When you throw water at others, you are bound to get wet yourself." When you spew hate on others, you are bound to keep most of it for yourself. This is not a way to create a healthy family or a good environment for children.

When you come into a blended family or when you are dealt a blended family, it can be a blessing if you add love to it. Decades ago, blended families were a taboo. If you had children out of wedlock, some families never spoke about it. So many children were raised without knowing who their parents were. Today, this is inexcusable. No child should be a secret. The affair and resulting mistrust, betrayal, and infidelity are all separate issues that need to be addressed, however, the children should not be punished for the situation. It takes strong people to deal with these difficult situations. If you can do it, it may be the greatest blessing of your life.

The same advice applies to a man if his wife commits adultery and has a child. Everything I said in this chapter applies. I know this is challenging for men even more so than women for all of the ego reasons that go along with an affair. However, if you decide to stay and work it out, then you owe the child your love as if the child is your own. Again, the child should not be subject to your pain and disappointment in your partner.

This chapter is not about should you stay or should you leave your spouse. This chapter is to make sure you understand that all children have a right to know their siblings so they may develop necessary relationships.

I know of what I speak, my father had a son from his first wife. I remember my father wanted to have a relationship with him and spoke about him often. Growing up, I can remember hearing conversations that my brother's mother would not let my dad see him and therefore he was kept out of our lives. I know my dad was a kind man and he was good to us. Again, I do not know the reason why we did not know this brother growing up. What I do know is something happened to cause the adults not to give us the opportunity to grow up together as family. This is a sad thing to do with children.

I missed out on the opportunity to get to know my brother, his wife, and his children. My brother's mom I never had a chance to meet, so when she passed away, we were not able to give my brother the support he so deserved. When his children were born, we did not get to know our nephews. When my dad died, this brother came to the funeral and heard all of the wonderful things we said about his own father. I remember him saying he wished he could have gone back and done things differently. The two people who were the cause of us not having a sibling relationship, both of them, are dead and gone now, leaving us to pick up the pieces and create a relationship that should have been encouraged and nurtured. I missed my brother's high school graduation, college graduation, wedding, birth of his children, holidays, etc. He missed all of mine. Do you know who got the raw end of the deal? We the children.

I am blessed now to be building a relationship with my brother which we continue to work on intentionally.

To use your children to make a point or to punish your ex by refusing them the right to develop and parent their child is not good. This has the potential to backfire on you and could hurt your children in the future.

Next, let's look at the ex-husband or ex-wife who gets married again and has additional children. Should you allow your children to have a relationship with those kids? Absolutely! Those children are a part of your children's life and you should not try to keep them apart for all of the reason I've previously stated. Is this a hard thing to do? Yes. The only way to avoid this situation is to remain faithfully married to one person for a life time. Unfortunately, this is not the exception but the norm in today's society. In some cases, you may have to deal with more than one person. This is why you have to look at the entire family dynamics. The traditional family as we know it is no longer the rule. Blended families are now the majority and no longer the minority.

I knew a man who was married with a new born baby and had a child from a previous relationship. That relationship lasted three years and, while it did not result in marriage, it did produce a two year old son. To complicate matters more the woman had a daughter who was now five years old. Newly married, he went to visit his two year old son, however, because the five year old girl knows him as the only father who has been in her life, she expected to go with him like always. The new wife could tolerate the man picking up his son, but she did not want anything to do with the other woman's five year old girl in spite of the relationship her husband had with the child for the last three years. Do you see how complicated this can become? This little girl did not ask for him to be invited into her life, yet this man asked this little girl to trust him as a father figure.

Here is what I believe should happen in this difficult situation. The man owes it to this girl to continue loving her because he invited her to invest in him emotionally. When he moved into the home, he essentially said to this little girl, "I am here for you and will cover you as a father." To pull completely out of her life could be devastating. His new wife should understand that when you bring someone into your life, you receive all of the baggage tied to them. (Let me be very clear; children are not nor should they be seen as baggage.) Children are little people who did not ask for or deserve the complications of adult relationships. You cannot request your partner to cut all ties with the children who are impacted by his or her life.

I would like to address an issue I've seen numerous times. Let me speak to the women who would make such a request to cut off children from a previous relationship. For the sake of dialogue we will call your partner Rick, Rick and you had a child together unfortunately the relationship did not work out. Now Rick finds a new partner named Betty and she asks him not to have anything to do with his child but to send him financial support. What would you think of Rick if he followed through with that request from Betty his new partner? You would think he was a man of no integrity and you would despise him as a father. What does a man look like fathering your baby and walking off, leaving you to raise the child by yourself?

A father loves his children, invests in his children, and spends time with his children. A father goes to see his children perform in school, meet their teachers, helps them with their homework, and counsels them through life. He is there for his children until that day he dies. This is my point to the women who make this request—if you meet a new gentleman and you ask him to walk away from his responsibility because you have insecurities about his past relationships, you might not be ready to enter into this relationship. I suggest you heal from your past hurts before you date anyone. Besides, any man that grants you this request will ultimately walk away from his responsibilities to you. A real man would *never* agree to these terms. If a man will walk away from his children, what good would he be to you and yours?

Children should never be punished for the breakup of their parents. Once you commit to care for a child as your own, you owe it to them to love them for a lifetime. You must think about this before you decide to get involved in another child's life and break hearts by walking away. When new partners come together, each must take everything that comes with the other person. Your children are my children, your family is my family, and we are all one, huge family. When blended with love, this new reality can work out to be a blessing to all involved.

CHAPTER 12

Outside Family Support

"The written word can be erased–not so with the spoken word."
Author Unknown

When we make a decision about our lives, many of us take very little advice from those we say we care about. We believe it is our life and we have a right to do with it as we please. However, when we make our decisions, we often expect everyone to agree with them. The truth is you certainly are able to have a relationship and marry whomever you want, but know your decision is just that—your decision. It would be kind if your family approved of your choices, however, your choice is your choice. It is not the choice of your mother, father, sisters, brothers, or friends.

Understand this, support from your immediate family is vital to the success of your blended family. Realistically this may not happen. Those who love you the most can often see things you may not see. So be patient with those who have your best interests in mind.

One of the mistakes people make in a blended family is sharing what you dislike about your mate and the bonus children with your family. When you do this, they form the same opinion about them based on what you tell them. However, as time moves on your thoughts and feelings may change but your family may still holding on to what you shared. Now you want them to receive someone you painted a bad picture of and they won't give him or her the time of day. If you desire the support of your family, be mindful of the things you share.

Let's look at your parents in relation to your blended family and the great benefit they will be to your children. Here are my thoughts on grandparents. Grandparents are God's gifts to children; they were created by God to love and spoil children. Grandparents are going to spoil their babies and to ask them not to would be unnatural. Grandparents live for this moment and they want only to give love with very little or no discipline. They will give your children things you don't want them to have and let them do the things you could not get away with growing up.

I know what you are saying about your parents: "Who are these people? I could never get away with what my children get away with." Grandparents are needed so children will feel pure, unadulterated, unconditional love. Children need a place where they can run and hide from the pains of life.

This may come as a surprise, As you have made life choices, you now receive everything that comes with the decisions. However, your mother and father did not ask for or should they be forced to accept or agree. This includes who you choose to be your new life partner.

Sure, it would be nice if your parents approve, but this may not be the case. You get a chance to pick whomever you want, however, other people have a right to reject your choice. When you invite a person into your life and that person brings other children with them, the grandparents have a right to receive your new family or not. Grandparents have their own lives to live and should not have the responsibilities of raising your children. Even your biological kids should not be forced on your parents.

I was in the store and met a grandmother who was around seventy years old with two young children about five and six years of age. She volunteered that her daughter did not want her children anymore and she just walked off and left them with her. So often in my lifetime I have seen men and women leave their kids for their mother or other family members to take care of. There is a reason why our

Creator made it possible for young people to have children; it's because they have the strength to handle it. When you have raised your children, it is unfair to be forced to do what is the responsibility of your adult children to do. (If you by chance are reading this book and your parents or family members are taking care of your children, I pray you will reevaluate this decision.)

Maybe some grandparents want to take on this responsibility, however, everyone should have the choice. I have never met any grandparent who wanted to do it, but I have met many who had to do it. Children want to be raised by their own parents. No matter how great a grandparent is to a child, he or she cannot substitute for or replace a parent. No one and nothing can take the place of a parent's love. When parents are unable to fulfill their duties, the children are forever scarred by the neglect. I have seen this happen in so many families and the kids suffer tremendously.

Grandparents have a right to enjoy their lives and should spend time with their grandchildren when they choose. I love hanging around my grandchildren. I want to hang around them all of the time. I get a real kick out of them and I am always excited to spend time with them. To me, this is what being a grandparent is all about. However, all I have done with my grandchildren has been by choice and not by force. If it was by force, I may not have enjoyed it so much. I understand that grandchildren are supposed to be God's reward for being a responsible parent. If you have a great parents, please do not rob them from having the opportunity to enjoy their grandchildren by choice. Every person is different, however, I believe the children truly benefit when they are welcomed.

Additionally, one of the worse things you can do is withhold your kids to punish your parents for not giving into your demands. I have seen where a daughter or son will use their children as hostages against the grandparents. In this situation, the grandparents are not allowed to see the grandchildren for not agreeing with their adult children's decisions. Grandchildren should never be used this way; it is a cruel thing to do to your parents.

Years ago, I knew a young lady whose mother was paying her rent as she worked to become established. She had a baby girl her mother just adored and the mother lavished her granddaughter with lots of gifts. The daughter could not afford daycare so the mother was kind enough to watch the baby while her daughter went to work. She became very attached to the girl. After a time, the grandmother noticed her daughter had become comfortable in not paying her rent. The daughter had received a raise from her job and hadn't mentioned the increase. The young lady started traveling and taking a few vacations a year. When the mother decided to make her daughter responsible and told her she was going to stop paying her rent, the daughter became very upset.

She told her mother she was placing the baby in day-care immediately and would no longer need her assistance. The daughter also said she was going to have to move and get another job. She told her mother she would be looking for another job out of town because she was not making enough to stay in the same city. This would mean the grandmother relationship with her granddaughter would be severed. The daughter knew very well how much her mother loved the baby and played on these emotions to get her mother to continue to pay the rent. The mother gave in to her daughter so she could continue to see her grand-daughter. The daughter had used the baby as a pawn to get what she wanted.

There was another person I knew whose name was Donald. Donald and Barbara weren't married and in time had a baby boy. Although Donald and Barbara had the baby out of wedlock, Donald's mother adored her only grandson. As life would have it, Donald and Barbara departed ways and Barbara denied Donald's family from seeing the baby.

The grandmother was heartbroken and pleaded with Barbara to change her mind. Barbara told Donald's mother that he was not paying child support and if she could speak to Donald concerning his responsibility, she would allow the baby to visit. This is a case of holding the baby hostage to try and manipulate a certain situation. (Again, if you are reading this book, and find yourself in a similar situation please reconsider, you're hurting your family) The grandmother and child should not be penalized for the behavior of the parents. The financial support of the child should be addressed through the court system; to use your children would be manipulation.

Allow me to share a few more stories, I knew of another situation where a man named Jay had a baby out of wedlock with Alice who already had one child before she met Jay. This situation was a little more complicated. The couple went to family functions with both children. The grandmother enjoyed time spending with her biological grandchild, and was very kind to Alice's other child as well. As time would have it, Jay and Alice departed ways and a year later Alice was married to Ray. Ray and Alice give birth to another child, so now Alice had three children with three different men.

Jay's mother wanted to spend time with her grandson and Alice made a demand that in order for Jay's son to come over, Jay's mother must take all of the children or she could not see any of them. Her rationale was when Jay's son came home from his grandmother's house, he had gifts that were unfair to the other children whose grandmothers were not involved. Here again is a case of holding the baby hostage to try and manipulate a certain situation.

Let me address this situation concerning grandparents taking on your bonus children from your new relationship. Even if the son, Jay, made the request that his mother take all of the children, it wouldn't matter. I believe grandparents, uncles, and aunts are not required to support you in the decision you have made concerning your new partner. They are under no obligation to accept or receive the decisions you make for your life. It is nice if they do support you and the new family, however, it should be their choice.

Parenting is your responsibility, grand parenting is strictly a choice. If I want to see my grandchildren, that is my decision to make. If I don't want to be bothered this weekend, I have a right to say no to seeing them. Let's go one step further. If I have a choice not to deal with my biological grandchildren, you know I don't have to deal with my bonus grandchildren. The drama that often comes with a blended family sometimes can be too much for our parents to bear. They should be able to enjoy their lives without any pressure. You did not seek the approval of your parents to marry them or have a child with them, so you don't get the opportunity to demand they form a relationship with your children or bonus children.

Here are a few reasons why your parents may not be as supportive as you like.

1. If your parents are not fond of the person you have chosen to begin a new family with.

   Solution: Your new partner can help in this area by winning them over with love. He or she should not use the line "I married you, not your family." Your goal is to have a successful bended family so your partner must do the work to win over your parents and family if possible.

2. Your parents may be attached to the previous partner and they are not ready to let them go as family.

   Solution: Let them know your ex can still remain a part of their family, however, you have moved on and would like them to receive the person now in your life. Talk to them about your happiness and see if they will support your journey. As you rebuild your life with your new partner, the new partner should come into the family showing a lot of love toward everyone. In time, your family's heart will turn towards the person you have chosen. This will take some time; it is not a short process.

3. If this is your third, fourth, or fifth marriage, your family will have a little trouble trusting your ability to pick a partner.

   Solution: You have to understand your family has built a wall so they won't become hurt again. They may choose to sit out your relationship emotionally until they see how stable it really is. Unfortunately, this has nothing to do with your new partner, but everything to do with you. The family will most likely be distant until they trust the relationship over time. Your partner should show love even though it may not be returned at this moment. You have to assure your partner the family is reacting to you and not them. Your partner will be a big help if he or she does not push the issue with your family. The best thing they can do is stay consistent and committed to loving you; the family should warm up to them in time.

Let's discuss what happens during a blended family Christmas concerning outside support. Christmas time is a huge challenge in my own family, though we love celebrating the day. When my children were young, we had to learn how to navigate through this day. We had four children who counted gifts to see if they had as much as each other. You can't purchase one child a Playstation 4 and give the second child a puzzle. You have to get kids gifts equal in value or status. Let's say, for instance, your two biological children's grandmother, aunts, and uncle purchase eight additional gifts for those two children. You should purchase eight addition gifts for your bonus children if possible to make all things fair. We spoke with everyone in the family to learn what the plan was for Christmas gifts. If one child was getting more, we made the adjustment before Christmas day so all of the children would feel good. Really try hard to balance the gifts out between all of the children so no one will feel badly.

This happens also during birthdays. If a biological child gets a huge birthday party, you have to make sure your bonus children receive the same. Children keep score with the other children, so be very careful to be fair and teach them what it means to have balance.

Concerning taking the children on an outing, it would be a good thing if the grandparents take all of the kids on the trip; it will cut down on a lot of problems. However, if they choose to take only the biological children, ask them what activities they will be doing. You should then take the other children and try to create something comparable so that when all the kids come home, they all have something to share about their day. Grandparents have a right to spend their money on who and what they want. They can buy a gift for one child or all of them; it is their choice. This is not the way it is in all cases.

If you find yourself in the situation where the grandparents are showing favoritism, take a breath sit down as a family, and have a heart to heart talk with the bonus children. Reassuring them how much you love them and how important they are to the family. If possible have a dialogue with your parents asking them to support your entire family. No one likes to be demanded to do anything, so talk about it and give your parents the options. Let them know it is not your intention to place them in any drama concerning your relationship. Ask them to pray about being more inclusive concerning all of the children. When you want people to accept what you are doing, include them in the decision process if possible.

Remember the people who love you want the best for you; give them the opportunity to share in your journey. Open your heart and something good will come from it. Love everybody and you have a chance for everybody to love you back.

CHAPTER 13

Taking Care of the Core

"There are two ways of being rich. One is to have all you want,
the other is to be satisfied with what you have."
Author Unknown

I n every family, the core revolves around the husband
and wife. They need to have a strong foundation of love,
respect, and support for one another in order for there to
be a chance for the family to thrive. I have yet to write
much about the love you must give your partner. As your
blended family develop, you should love and support each
other as husband and wife more, I believe, than in a traditional family. It is so critical to show your partner they are
the most important person to you, partly because you have
to deal with the exes.

There is a potential for a lot of jealousy and insecurity
to creep into your marriage. It is up to you to make sure

your husband or wife know you value their efforts in this relationship; keep reminding them of how much you love them. It takes a special person to take the pieces of a broken home and blend it together as one, especially with all the outside forces that come against a blended family. If you have found someone who understands, who is willing to do the hard work, and who puts forth the effort, then love them with everything within you. Such a person is hard to find and your marriage is worth the investment.

When I think about how to protect the core of the marriage and work in communion with your spouse, these words come to mind as good advice to follow:

Watch your thoughts, they become words;
watch your words, they become actions;
watch your actions, they become habits;
watch your habits, they become character;
watch your character, for it becomes your destiny.

One of the things you must guard against is the urge to quit and get a divorce. If you have been divorced one time before, it may be easier for you to do it again. I cannot stress it enough, you must stay committed. You should take divorce off the table; if you leave it on the table, you will take the option sooner or later.

I spoke to a young man who believed his wife did not show appreciation for all of the hard work he was contributing to make the blended family work. When speaking to the wife, she felt she shows him all the time how much she appreciates him. What I have found so often with couples is a serious miscommunication. To combat this, I came up with an exercise I want you to try if you ever feel unappreciated by each other. I normally do not like keeping score in a marriage, however, for the sake of this exercise, I will have you do so.

Here's how the exercise works. Every time you do something you consider to be special for your partner, give them an I appreciate you ticket. For example, you run your wife's bathwater. You will give her a ticket. Let's say your wife presses your shirt. She should give you the shirt along with a ticket of appreciation.

When this exercise is done consistently, again I don't believe in keeping score in a marriage but it may be easy to see you really are appreciated. In time you won't need this exercise, the results can be eye-opening.

This brings me to the second part of the exercise. Let's say your husband ran your bathwater and gave you an appreciation ticket. If you feel the act should be perceived as a normal act, then you have a right to receive the ticket, but voice "I see this as normal." The reason you need to do this is because someone may feel they are appreciating you with special attention and, if you see it as normal, it will not register. The other person will be loving on you and you will not recognize it. This is what happened in this couple's relationship. The husband could not recognize the special appreciation his wife was giving him because he saw it as normal while she saw it as appreciation. The wife would fix his lunch for work every day and the husband would pick it up off the counter without giving it a second thought. He did not see the love being show to him by fixing his lunch.

The exercise should continue for two weeks. You will be surprised what the other person is doing to show you appreciation and how you may see it differently. You may also find out something else, such as you may be so busy with everyday life that you are not doing enough to appreciate each other. If you go two or three days without taking out the time to hug, kiss, and love on your partner, your marriage is going to have problems. You should pour back into each other on a daily bases if your blended family is going to work. By regularly giving tickets of appreciation, you can see and track how you are paying attention to the most important person in your life.

If someone tells you fixing their lunch is not showing them the appreciation they need, then stop, ask them what they need to feel your love. If you keep fixing the person lunch, and they are telling you that this is not what they need to feel appreciated, it will not fulfill the need of you or your partner. I suggest you go online and take the test to find out your partner's love language. You can do twenty things a person sees as normal and do two things the person sees as special and they will be happy with the two things. Upon learning that, drop the twenty things and just work on what makes your partner feel appreciated.

After the couple I was counseling did this exercise, they both were surprised how way off they were from what the other person needed to feel loved. He was picking up his bonus kids every day from school thinking his wife saw it as something special. She saw this as normal and did not give it a second thought. However, because he is the bonus dad, he was making a special effort to love his bonus children as his own and she needs to acknowledge this effort. Loving her children is normal to the mom because they are her children, but in the eyes of the bonus dad, he is making a special effort to be a great dad.

Both parties must take the time to make sure the other is shown love, and receives that love, if you want to have a strong blended family. Give your spouse what he or she needs and you will get back what you need. In this way you both will have the strength to do the work necessary to build your blended family.

CHAPTER 14

Committed to the Blended Family

"One thing you can give and still keep is your word."
Author Unknown

As with any family, you have to make a commitment to the blended family and renew your love for one another over and over again. If all involved are not giving 100%, it will take a toll on the family. The work in any marriage, traditional or blended, requires your full attention. Children will not see your sacrifices as clearly as you would like, however, in time they will reflect back over their lives and began to see the hard work it took for their family to be successful. Sometimes this does not happen until they have their own families, so don't be discouraged when you don't receive the response back you feel you deserve.

I am reminded of a family that adopted a child from foster care and gave her a home. In that home, the girl received her own room, a closet full of clothes, and a place in private school. The parent felt the adopted daughter should have been tremendously grateful for their sacrifices. However, children, for the most part, do not rationalize or navigate through the process of appreciation. They are so consumed with their needs they are not usually concerned about your feelings. This is not on purpose; it is the way young people process things. Most time you will not receive any accolade for many years to come. In any event, remain committed to the process.

Here's what has helped me during these times. I stopped looking at the person I was making the sacrifice for and I started doing it for my heavenly Father. I often refer to Matthew 25:31-40 (NKJV).

> When the Son of Man comes in His glory, and all the holy angels with Him, then He will sit on the throne of His glory. All the nations will be gathered before Him, and He will separate them one from another, as a shepherd divides his sheep from the goats. And He will set the sheep on His right hand, but the goats on the left. Then the King will say to those on His right

hand, "Come, you blessed of My Father, inherit the kingdom prepared for you from the foundation of the world: for I was hungry and you gave Me food; I was thirsty and you gave Me drink; I was a stranger and you took Me in; I was naked and you clothed Me; I was sick and you visited Me; I was in prison and you came to Me."

Then the righteous will answer Him, saying, "Lord, when did we see You hungry and feed You, or thirsty and give You drink? When did we see You a stranger and take You in, or naked and clothe You? Or when did we see You sick, or in prison, and come to You?" And the King will answer and say to them, "Assuredly, I say to you, inasmuch as you did it to one of the least of these My brethren, you did it to Me."

Think about it. When you have done it to the least of these—the children— you have done it unto Me. When I feel I am not being appreciated for my work on the behalf of my family, I don't quit doing the hard work. I do it now unto my heavenly Father and look to Him to reward me and pay me back in ways my family would never be able to do. I stay committed to getting the job done. At some point and time, those who you are loving on will see your sacrifices and give you the proper recognition so stay the course.

Family is the most important entity in life. You must love, forgive, apologize, and laugh a lot if you are going to make it. Give room for people to make mistakes and give people room to grow. There is a wide range of emotions displayed on a daily bases by everyone involved in the family dynamics. One day you may have to extend patience to the parents, the next day to the children, and still another day to the ex spouses. Do everything you can to understand the why behind people's behaviors and try not to react without wisdom. Don't be afraid to seek godly counsel from someone who understands the dynamics of a blended family. Give lots of love to the children and remember they did not ask to be here; this was your choice. Children, bonus and biological, need and deserve special love and support from you.

When a blended family is strong and when you invest the time to get it right, it can have great benefits. Some of my family's greatest joys are the times we spent together when we didn't have a big house or a lot of money. What we did have was a lot of love to give to our children and each other. Do you know love is the greatest gift you can give to your family? If you continue to show love, I can guarantee there will be no issue you will not be able to overcome. We all need love to survive; if you don't have love in your family, there is no strategy that will save it. You can have the biggest house, drive the nicest car, make all the money in the world, but none of these things will satisfy you. Love is the key to building a healthy family. Love is not born out of lust, it is born out of commitment. The more you invest in your marriage, the more the love will grow. I love my wife more today than I did when we first met. Whatever you invest in is where your heart will be. The bible said in Matthew 6:21 (NKJV) "wherever your treasure is there will your heart be also." The more you invest into your family, the greater the treasure and your heart will follow.

CHAPTER 15

Conclusion

"Always end the day with a positive thought. No matter how hard things were, tomorrow's a fresh opportunity to make it better."
Unknown Author

As we come to the close of this book, I pray I have helped you with some of the concerns your blended family may be dealing with. Make no mistake about it, I repeat, blended families are very hard work and, in some cases, much more difficult than a traditional family. If you can get all of the horses pulling in the same direction, however, a blended family can be a beautiful thing.

As a man thinks in his heart, so he is. You must think of your blended family as blessed and blessing will flow through your family. In my family, we decided to keep God first; we placed our faith in Jesus Christ above all else. We follow the Christian principles the bible lays out. Prayer, faith, love, and forgiveness have helped us get through very difficult times. We could not have made it without the help of our Lord and Savior, Jesus Christ.

What I can tell you is no matter what race, color, or country, blended families take a lot of love and work. Those who have done it well should be given much respect and credit for succeeding. That is what I want to say in this last chapter—I want to celebrate everyone that has hung in there and made it to the other side. Joining your life to another person for life sounds beautiful, but you have to reinvent your marriage over and over again. So hats off to the people who have found a way to blend a family and make it work.

I also want to celebrate all the men and women who have made the commitment to be an excellent bonus parent to their bonus children. You have learned to make huge scarifies for your family. One of the most challenging jobs in the world is to love children when they are not being lovable. To you who have allowed a child into your home after an affair, huge kudos to you for putting your hurts and pains in the background for the sake of the child. To all the biological parents, thank you for allowing the bonus parents to share in the lives of your children.

What can I say about the children who give the blended family a chance? Thank you for allowing us bonus parents to rent space in your heart. We forget the things children have to endure and the pain they feel from the loss of their initial home and surroundings. A huge congratulations to all of the children from blended families who have come out on the other side as productive adults.

I hope this book has helped you in some way understand the journey before you as a blended family. May the Lord bless and keep you, and help you to love a lot, laugh a lot, and use wisdom in all things. Family is and always will be the most important entity on earth. Take it seriously; your family is valuable. Family is God's gift to you for better or for worse, for richer or for poorer, in sickness and in health, to love and to cherish, till death do you part. Blessing and favor be upon you as you meet the challenges that come with a blended family. I speak this into your life—victory shall be yours in area every.... AMEN!

CPSIA information can be obtained
at www.ICGtesting.com
Printed in the USA
LVOW03s0704070917
547806LV00001B/2/P

9 781498 493390